VINÍCIUS JÚNIOR

MATT AND TOM OLDFIELD

ULTIMATE
FOOTBALL HEROES

VINÍCIUS
JÚNIOR

FROM THE PLAYGROUND
TO THE PITCH

DINO

First published by Dino Books in 2023,
an imprint of Bonnier Books UK,
4th Floor, Victoria House, Bloomsbury Square, London WC1B 4DA
Owned by Bonnier Books,
Sveavägen 56, Stockholm, Sweden

X @UFHbooks
X @footieheroesbks
www.heroesfootball.com
www.bonnierbooks.co.uk

Text © Matt Oldfield 2023
The right of Matt Oldfield to be identified as the author of this work has been
asserted by him in accordance with the Copyright, Designs and Patents Act 1988.

Design by www.envydesign.co.uk

Paperback ISBN: 978 1 78946 493 1
E-book ISBN: 978 1 78946 501 3

British Library cataloguing-in-publication data:
A catalogue record for this book is available from the British Library.

Printed and bound in Great Britain by Clays Ltd, Elcograf S.p.A.

5 7 9 10 8 6 4

For all readers,
young and old(er)

ULTIMATE
FOOTBALL HEROES

Matt Oldfield is a children's author focusing on the wonderful
world of football. His other books include *Unbelievable Football*
(winner of the 2020 Children's Sports Book of the Year) and the
Johnny Ball: Football Genius series. In association with his
writing, Matt also delivers writing workshops in schools.

Cover illustration by Dan Leydon.
To learn more about Dan visit danleydon.com
To purchase his artwork visit etsy.com/shop/footynews
Or just follow him on X @danleydon

TABLE OF CONTENTS

ACKNOWLEDGEMENTS

First of all I'd like to thank everyone at Bonnier Books for supporting me and for running the ever-expanding UFH ship so smoothly. Writing stories for the next generation of football fans is both an honour and a pleasure. Thanks also to my agent, Nick Walters, for helping to keep my dream job going, year after year.

Next up, an extra big cheer for all the teachers, booksellers and librarians who have championed these books, and, of course, for the readers. The success of this series is truly down to you.

Okay, onto friends and family. I wouldn't be writing this series if it wasn't for my brother Tom. I owe him so much and I'm very grateful for his belief in me as an author. I'm also very grateful to the rest of my family, especially Mel, Noah, Nico, and of course Mum and Dad. To my parents, I owe my biggest passions: football and books. They're a real inspiration for everything I do.

Pang, Will, Mills, Doug, Naomi, John, Charlie, Sam, Katy, Ben, Karen, Ana (and anyone else I forgot) – thanks for all the love and laughs, but sorry, no I won't be getting 'a real job' anytime soon!

And finally, I couldn't have done any of this without Iona's encouragement and understanding. Much love to you, and of course to Arlo, the ultimate hero of all. I hope we get to enjoy these books together one day.

CHAPTER 1

CHAMPIONS LEAGUE HERO

28 May 2022, Stade de France

When Vinícius Jr.'s alarm went off that morning, he reached across for his phone and checked his messages as if it was any other day. Except it wasn't. Tonight would be the 2022 Champions League final and he was in France preparing for the biggest game of his life.

He sat up and stretched, shrugging off the nervous feeling in his stomach. Ever since signing with Real Madrid, 'Vini' had dreamed of winning the Champions League. It was the trophy that everyone talked about – and the photos were plastered on the walls at the stadium, at the training ground and in just about every other corridor he could remember. Zinedine Zidane. Raul. Luís Figo. Cristiano Ronaldo. Sergio Ramos. The list went on and on. So many Real Madrid legends had won that giant silver cup.

Vini put on his Real tracksuit and took the lift down to the huge hotel lobby. As the doors opened, he grinned at the familiar sight in the doorway of the team's meeting room. Real manager Carlo Ancelotti had the same calm face as always, and Vini immediately felt better. Carlo's belief in him had turned around his Real experience.

Once all the players had found a seat, Carlo and the coaches went through further instructions, using the big TV screens on the back wall. 'We know Liverpool are going to press us in midfield,' Carlo explained, looking at Luka Modrić and Toni Kroos. 'But we can play around it – just get the ball out to Vini as often as you can.'

All the reporters were talking about Vini's battle with Trent Alexander-Arnold, and he knew that the Liverpool right-back was great going forward but could sometimes lose concentration when forced to defend. Vini listened carefully, but the clock in the meeting room seemed to be ticking more slowly than ever. He just wanted to get out on the pitch with a ball at his feet.

While the players left the room, picking up bottles of water on their way out, Vini stopped next to the whiteboard that showed the timing for the team bus ride to the stadium.

Carlo appeared out of nowhere. 'This is your moment,' he said, putting an arm round Vini. 'It's what you've worked so hard for. Now go and enjoy it!'

Vini laughed. He still remembered his first talks with Carlo and how he'd left the room each time feeling ten feet tall. All along, his manager had given him the freedom to be himself on the pitch. That meant playing with a smile and taking on defenders.

It was still hours before kick-off, but Vini could hear the screams of a large crowd of Real fans outside the hotel. As he boarded the bus, with his headphones tucked under his arm, he waved to them.

There were Real fans lining the streets along the way, smiling and laughing. Almost all of them were wearing the club's famous white shirt.

During the warm-up for the game, Vini jogged over to join a circle of his teammates and flicked the ball around. His touch felt sharp as he moved from side to side – and standing next to Luka and Karim Benzema, he felt more confident that the night would end with the Champions League trophy in his hands.

'These finals are why we play the game,' Luka said, grinning. As usual, he was barely sweating. 'There's nothing else like it.'

Luka would know, Vini thought. He had already won the trophy four times.

Somehow the VINI JR 20 Real shirt, hanging in the dressing room, looked even more spectacular that night. Vini could feel the history and successes – and now he was following in the club legends' giant footsteps.

'It's almost time,' Carlo said quietly as the whole dressing room turned to listen. 'Everything about our journey to the final has felt magical. We were counted out against Chelsea and again when we were losing to Manchester City. But we don't quit.'

Vini nodded as he taped his ankles.

In the tunnel, he closed his eyes, took a deep breath and said a quiet prayer. At last, he heard the tap-tap of studs on the tunnel floor and the line started moving. The Champions League anthem blared out from the loudspeakers as Vini walked out onto the perfect green pitch.

'Let's go!' Karim shouted, high-fiving Vini on his way for the coin toss.

After the first few minutes, Vini felt the nerves disappear and his focus shifted to helping his team win the game. The first half was tight and no-one wanted to make a big mistake.

'Just stick to the plan,' Carlo said at half-time. 'We're exactly where we want to be, and the chances will come. But when we get the ball wide, we've got to get more support in the box for Karim.'

In the second half, Real found their rhythm. A neat move on the right gave Federico Valverde some space. He took a quick touch and glanced up to check his options. Vini remembered Carlo's half-time words and rushed forward to support him.

Vini had played with Federico for years – from the Castilla reserve team all the way to the Real first team – and he could guess what was coming next. When Federico swung his right foot to whip the ball across the box, Vini was already on the move.

He timed his run perfectly, reacting faster than Alexander-Arnold. Vini's eyes lit up as Federico's cross-shot flew away from Allison, the Liverpool goalkeeper, and into his path. He slowed down just enough to side foot a quick shot into the net. *1–0!*

Gooooooooooooooooooooaaaaaaaaaaaaaaaaalllllllllllllllllllllllllll!!!!!!!!!!!!!!!!!!!!

Vini raced away towards the fans, grabbing the Real badge on his shirt and flashing his trademark smile. Was this really happening?! The crowd's reaction gave him a clear answer. Vini could hardly hear his teammates as they raced over and jumped on his back. But Vini knew Liverpool wouldn't give up. He focused on getting back and helping the midfield. His heart skipped a beat a few times whenever Thibaut Courtois dived to make key saves.

He watched the final seconds from the bench, after a standing ovation from the fans and a hug from Carlo. Then it was all over! Vini leapt into the air and rushed onto the pitch to celebrate with his teammates.

'We did it!' he yelled, hugging Karim and Luka. Standing in the line for his medal, Vini caught a glimpse of the shiny Champions League trophy. Real had won it as a team, but it still felt great to score the winning goal.

The past few years had been a whirlwind for Vini, with many highlights but some challenges and bumps. But now he really believed that anything was possible. He was still only twenty-one and he was just getting started.

CHAPTER 2

SÃO GONÇALO'S GOLDEN BOY

As Little Vini looked out of the window, he saw a group of older boys making a goal with old milk cartons for posts. A scuffed, muddy ball pinged from one foot to the next when the boys ran around in the São Gonçalo street. It looked like fun!

With his focus on the football game, what Vini didn't see in that moment was the difficult surroundings in São Gonçalo – the dirty water, the rubbish on the ground and the lack of food. But he was already old enough to know that São Gonçalo could be dangerous.

His parents, Vinícius and Fernanda, had settled in this big, crowded neighbourhood, within the city of

Rio de Janeiro. They made the most of their family time, but life was hard.

There was a loud noise from just up the street, and Fernanda joined her son at the window nervously, looking left and right. The older boys had rushed off. They couldn't see anything, but Fernanda still guided Vini away from the window.

When Vini's parents weren't worrying about staying safe in São Gonçalo, they had money challenges to think about. There were so few jobs, and they had bills to pay.

'What are we going to do?' Fernanda asked, looking at her husband. 'How are we going to give our kids a better life?'

Vinícius didn't know. He hugged his wife. It would take a miracle.

'We'll find a way,' he said. 'Keep believing.'

'Always!' she said, smiling bravely and glancing over at their children. Vini was sitting on the floor next to his sister Alessandra and little brother Netinho.

The first task for Vinícius was finding a job. After

weeks of searching, he got one, but it wasn't in São Gonçalo. Every bit of good news seemed to have bad news attached to it. Now he would be away and would miss precious moments with his children.

As usual, they found a way to make it work, with help from the rest of the family. Sitting at the table one weekend, Vinícius and Fernanda were thankful for getting to the end of another long week.

'Coming through!' Vini called suddenly, whizzing past them with his little ball and almost tripping on a chair leg.

But he kept his balance, weaving in and out in the tiny space. When he got to the front door, he turned around and did the same run back through the house.

'Have you seen the way he dribbles his ball around?' Fernanda said, turning to her husband. 'Football could be his route out of here to a better life.'

'He's definitely a true Brazilian!' Vinícius replied, grinning. 'He loves watching the older kids playing in the street too. Before we know it, he'll be out there with them.'

There was a knock at the door, and Vinícius got up. 'That'll be Ulysses,' he said.

'Uncle Ulysses!' Vini shouted excitedly, after his dad had let him in.

Ulysses crouched down and tried to kick the ball away from Vini. But he was too slow. Vini spun around him laughing.

'The boy's got talent!' Ulysses said, giving up any hope of getting the ball. 'Have you looked at registering him for one of the local youth teams? There's only a very small fee and it'll keep him out of trouble.'

Vinícius and Fernanda looked at each other, smiling. 'We were actually just talking about his love of football,' Fernanda said.

'Well, think about it,' Ulysses replied. 'If you're interested, I can ask a few friends for suggestions on the local teams.'

'Yes please!' Vini called, rushing past them on another run. They all laughed.

When Ulysses got up to leave, Vini appeared out

of nowhere, tapping the ball through his uncle's legs. 'Got you!' he said, giggling.

Hugging Vini at the door, Ulysses grinned. 'I'm always telling your parents that you're welcome to come and stay with me any time,' he said. 'I'll be working on my goalie skills so I'm ready for you.'

Vini smiled. He liked going to see Uncle Ulysses and Auntie Tatiana. 'You're on!' he said.

CHAPTER 3

LEARNING FROM CACAU

There were plenty of football schools and academies to choose from across Rio de Janeiro, and Vini's family wanted to be sure that they picked one that was the right fit for him. Ulysses got a recommendation from a friend to try the Escolinha de Flamengo.

Coach Carlos Eduardo Abrantes, or 'Cacau', was in charge there. He had seen hundreds of talented boys improve and thrive at his football school. It was a job he loved – setting the next generation of young players on the road to chasing their football dreams.

The boys' dreams were usually very similar: to play for one of the country's biggest clubs and to one day wear the famous yellow Brazil shirt. But only a handful of kids really stood a chance. Cacau's job was to help his group of boys improve each week.

While he carried the balls and cones over to the small pitch for that afternoon's training session, he spotted a little figure already dribbling a ball around – a flick, a few keepy ups, another flick, a quick change of direction, then a rocket shot.

The boy skipped over to get the ball, working on a goal celebration as he went.

Cacau smiled, recognising Vini, the new boy from last week. He was early for training again and working up a sweat in the hot sun.

Immediately, Cacau could see that the boy had some special skills. The ball barely left his foot as he weaved in and out – and he could dribble faster than some kids his age could run.

It only took a couple more training sessions for the coaches to huddle together in disbelief. Vini was unstoppable in the mini games. He had the pace to outrun all the other boys and he only needed a quick touch to leave them behind.

But when he got bored with that, Vini had all

the tricks. He dribbled left and right, he could do stepovers and turns at lightning speed, and he had the most powerful shot that Cacau had ever seen in this age group. How was he only seven?!

'Vini is a one-of-a-kind talent,' Cacau said as the coaches sat down together for a snack after training. 'I don't want to put too much pressure on him, but it feels like testing him against older boys is the right thing to do.'

'He's ready for it,' one of the other coaches added. 'The Under-9s will be perfect for him.'

Vini beamed when he heard the news. Cacau even had a backpack for him so that it was easier for him to bring his kit and boots to training.

'Okay, superstar, let's see what you've got!' Felipe, one of the Under-9s, said at the start of Vini's first session with the older boys. He was half-smiling, so Vini decided it was just a friendly joke. But he could tell that the boys were curious about why a seven-year-old was showing up at their practice.

Within minutes, they understood. Before the training session started, Vini had felt too shy to talk to the other boys, but that all changed once he had a ball at his feet.

'Play it back!' he yelled, sprinting across to create room for a pass.

'Knock it through!' he screamed, pointing to where he wanted the ball.

When Felipe won a tackle, the ball bounced loose, and Vini swooped in as if he had known in advance where it would land. In an instant, he was dribbling at full speed, shimmying away from one defender, swaying past another, then firing a low shot into the net.

Goooooooooooooooooooaaaaaaaaaaaaaaaaallllllllllllll llllllllllll!!!!!!!!!!!!!!!!!!!!

'Are you serious?' Felipe shouted, running over and jumping on Vini's back. 'Even Ronaldinho would have been proud of that one!'

Cacau had been watching from the far side of the pitch for the whole session. Somehow Vini looked even better against the Under-9s.

'Where did you find this kid?' the other parents asked. 'He's incredible!'

Cacau smiled. 'I taught him everything he knows,' he joked, pretending to do a few stepovers on the touchline.

But Vini was just getting started. After talking with Cacau, he stayed with the Under-9s for the rest of the season – and the goals kept flowing.

Though it was always a long journey to get to training and matches, Vini couldn't stop smiling.

'Thanks for making this possible, Mum,' he said as they got home one night. 'I know it's really tiring for you, but I'm so happy to be part of the team.'

Fernanda looked at him, with tears in her eyes. 'That's all I could ever want,' she said, hugging him tightly.

CHAPTER 4

A FUTSAL NATURAL

It was another scorching day in São Gonçalo. As Vini walked home from school with his friend Wesley, they had to stop every few minutes to wipe the sweat from their foreheads.

'It's so hot!' Vini said. 'It feels like my shirt is actually stuck to my body!' He tugged at his shirt and wriggled to unstick it from his skin.

'There's more shade down this street,' Wesley replied, pointing. At least there were a few shop signs that gave them some protection from the sun.

When they turned the corner, Wesley clapped his hands. 'Finally, a bench!' he said. 'Let's take a quick break.'

But Vini's attention had wandered. He could hear shouts and laughter coming from the nearest building, where the door had been left wide open.

He walked over cautiously and then peered inside.

'Wow, come and check this out!' he shouted. 'Futsal!'

Vini had already decided that he wanted to be the type of footballer who entertained the crowd with tricks, flicks and any other moves that got fans on their feet. He had heard a lot about futsal, but this was a rare chance to see it.

Watching the futsal game, Vini had never felt so alive. The ball flew from end to end on the small pitch. The boys were probably only a few years older than him, but they were all magicians with the ball at their feet. One dipped his shoulder and danced past a tackle. Another controlled the ball on his thigh and flicked a pass with his heel. Vini and Wesley just kept looking at each other in amazement.

When Vini heard that there were futsal teams for his age group, he knew he had to try it. Luckily, there was a local option and he signed up with the Canto do

Rio team.

It was just as much fun as he had expected, based on the twenty minutes he had seen with Wesley – and he was perfect for it. Vini had all the skills, but futsal improved his movement too. With the smaller pitch, he had to be even sharper with his runs and his control. Instead of keeping the ball and trying to trick his way past defenders, Vini got better and better at playing one-twos and darting into space.

There were many futsal teams scattered around the city and the battles were fierce. When he looked back on his first year with Canto do Rio, his favourite memory was a trick that even left his own teammates stunned. It had seemed like Vini had nowhere to go with two defenders blocking his path, but he grinned as the thought went through his head to try a move that he had been working on at home.

In a flash, he put one foot in front of the ball, with the other just behind it. Then he flicked the ball up over his head, over the nearest defender's head, and raced forward to reach it first. There were whistles and gasps from the players and coaches, but Vini ignored all that and crossed the ball for a tap-in.

He could still remember his teammates' faces. 'Whoa, no way!' they yelled, laughing. 'Where did that come from?!'

But as much as Vini enjoyed futsal, he was inching closer to the age for a trial to get into the Flamengo football youth academy. By that point, juggling football and futsal was becoming too much. He had a choice to make. He loved the freedom of futsal, but knew he would always regret it if he didn't give football his full attention.

'I'll just have to bring my futsal skills with me then,' Vini told his mum, grinning. 'That's the Brazilian way, isn't it?'

Fernanda laughed. 'Whatever you're playing, wherever you're playing, I have no doubt that you'll be entertaining anyone who's there,' she replied.

CHAPTER 5

TAKING THE FLAMENGO ACADEMY BY STORM

Vini put his boots in the backpack that Cacau had given him when he was in the Under-9s. 'Hopefully today is the day,' he said to Fernanda as they were leaving the house for his trial at Flamengo.

'Don't put too much pressure on yourself, darling,' Fernanda replied. 'Just play the way you always do.'

Vini nodded. His mum was right. The trial was just another game.

Vini's mouth dropped open when they arrived at the training centre. It looked incredible! He was only ten, but he felt like a professional as he walked into the building. One of the academy coaches met him near the entrance and led the way to the changing rooms at the back.

As usual, it took Vini a little time to get comfortable around the other boys. Some of them had clearly been at Flamengo for a few years already. After the warm-up and a few passing drills, they were split into groups for some 3-on-3 games on a small pitch marked out with red cones.

Vini was on the green team with two taller boys who introduced themselves as Joao and Miguel. He forced himself to speak up more. 'How long have you been at Flamengo?' he asked Joao as they were passing the ball to each other, waiting for the yellow team to come over.

'This is my second year,' Joao said. 'The coaches work us hard, but they like to have fun too.'

Before Vini could ask any more questions, the game was starting. One of the coaches blew a whistle and rolled the ball onto the pitch.

Vini knew he was now playing against some of the best young players in the whole of Brazil. But there was no time to get nervous about that. 'Just play!' he told himself.

At first, Vini took the safe options. He controlled a pass and knocked the ball back to Joao. When Miguel dribbled forward, Vini moved into space and called for a pass. He avoided one tackle and gave the ball back to Miguel. His touch felt good and he was showing that he knew the pass-and-move basics.

After the first drink break, Vini decided it was time to let loose a little. The coaches had seen that he could pass. Now he needed to show them what else he could do.

Joao fired a quick pass to Vini on the right side of the pitch. His marker was probably expecting Vini to do what he had done earlier in the game – a quick lay-off or a simple pass. But instead Vini flicked the ball with the inside of his right foot and spun to his left, leaving the defender stumbling after him.

Now he had room to dribble. He darted forward, faked to go right with a stepover and then sped to his left. Another yellow shirt rushed over, but Vini was flying. He shimmied one way and weaved the other, bursting through before the defender could recover. With one more touch, he smashed a shot into the tiny goal.

Goooooooooooooooooooaaaaaaaaaaaaaaaaallllllllllllll llllllllllll!!!!!!!!!!!!!!!!!!!!

That felt good! Vini's whole body seemed to be jumping with excitement, but he tried to play it cool as Joao and Miguel ran over.

'What a move!' Miguel shouted, ruffling Vini's hair. 'You turned them inside out.'

A few of the other coaches were paying attention now too at the side of the pitch. Vini decided to show them that last goal was no fluke.

He called for the ball again, dropping back next to Miguel. The yellow team had learned their lesson. One defender ran over, with another lurking nearby in case Vini started dribbling again.

Vini let the first defender get a little closer and then he started dribbling forward, but slower this time. 'Close him down!' called one of the yellow shirts. But when the defender began to lunge, Vini was ready. With his right foot, he scooped the ball over the defender's head and sprinted after it.

He looked up. Maybe he could take a shot, but the

angle was tight. The yellow shirts were all chasing back now, expecting him to dribble again or shoot. But, with a quick turn, Vini jinked back the other way and poked a pass through to Joao. He was all alone for a tap-in.

'Even Joao couldn't miss that!' Miguel called, patting Vini on the back. 'I want to be on your team every week!'

For the coaches, this was just about the easiest decision ever after a trial. Vini was the star of the session.

'You've got some magic feet there!' one of the coaches said, shaking Vini's hand as they sat down in one of the small rooms inside the training centre. 'That was an incredible performance and we're excited to see more.'

Vini nodded. This was sounding good! 'So, does that mean I can come to training next week as well?' He was sure that he could pass this trial if he had a few more games like tonight.

'Not just next week, Vini,' the coach said, smiling. 'We want you here every week. We've seen all we need to see for this trial. We want to sign you for the Flamengo academy.'

Vini almost fell off his chair. He put his hands over his face. This meant everything to him.

'Congratulations, young man,' the coach added, handing over some forms for Vini to bring home. 'We can't wait to have you at the club.'

Vini knew the hard work was only just starting, but first, it was time for a party. Vinícius Sr. and Fernanda beamed with pride when they heard the news, and Uncle Ulysses and Auntie Tatiana invited the family for a special meal to celebrate the moment.

As the months passed at Flamengo, the only challenge for Vini was the long journey for each training session. Of course, he would have walked for days to get this opportunity, but the travel back and forth from the academy was tiring out the whole family.

Then Uncle Ulysses had an idea. 'What do you think about Vini moving in with Tatiana and I during the week so he's much closer for training?' he asked Fernanda. 'We'd bring him home for the weekends.'

Fernanda thought about it. With her husband still working in another town, she was always trying to do a hundred things at once. It made her sad to think of Vini moving out – but it wouldn't be a permanent thing and he would still be living with family.

Vini had mixed feelings about it. He was excited to have a much shorter journey to training, but he worried about leaving his mum. 'I'll be back home every weekend,' he told her. 'But if you need me, call me any time!'

At Flamengo, the coaches were blown away each week by the latest tricks that Vini had added to his game. But once training was over, he was back to being a regular teenager. Sometimes that meant playing FIFA with his friends Wesley and Luiz; other times, he just enjoyed spending time with Uncle Ulysses and Auntie Tatiana.

His coaches kept pushing him – moving him up to play against older age groups at the Flamengo academy and helping him to combine his speed and skills with better movement and more accurate passing.

As one of the country's best young players, he was soon snapped up by a top agency. Now Vini had somewhere to turn when he had questions about the next steps in his career. At the same time, the agency helped his family too, making it easier for them to move closer to where Vini was training.

On the pitch, Vini was scoring every type of goal – right foot, left foot, volleys, tap-ins, even a few headers – and he was making it all look simple.

'How do you keep doing this?' Uncle Ulysses asked him one night. 'Most of the defenders are at least a year older than you, and sometimes two years older. But you leave them behind every time.'

Vini smiled. His coaches had given him the freedom to drift to the left wing or right wing to get on the ball, and he was always looking out for the weakest defender.

At the start of the season, most opponents didn't know much about him. 'Don't worry about the little guy,' he heard one coach call out.

But before long, Vini had a reputation around the league and he was the first Flamengo player that opponents worried about with their game plan. Instead of teams dismissing him as 'that little guy', the tackles got harder and defenders tried every trick to wind him up. Vini's response was usually a nutmeg or a stepover that left his marker on the ground.

His family watched in amazement. Vini was just taking it all in his stride. With more and more scouts showing up at Flamengo academy games, it would have been natural for Vini to either start getting nervous or letting all the attention go to his head. But neither happened. He was still just Vini.

'That's cool,' he always said when he heard stories about scouts and where his career might go. 'I'll just keep letting my football do the talking and we'll see what happens next.'

CHAPTER 6

COPINHA MAGIC

Vini continued to rise through the Flamengo academy and he was heading towards his toughest test yet.

'You know what happens in January, right?' his academy teammate Lincoln asked him, with a big smile as they walked onto the Flamengo training pitch.

Vini thought for a second, then he and Lincoln said together: 'The Copinha!'

It was all that some of the older age groups at Flamengo had talked about last year – a tournament that brought together the best Under-20 teams in Brazil. Even better, The Copinha also attracted scouts from across the country and some of the big clubs in Europe.

'Neymar and Gabriel Jesus put themselves on the map at the Copinha,' Vini said, picking up a ball from the pile.

'Aren't you nervous?' Lincoln asked, watching Vini smiling and working on his stepovers.

'Why? I'm just having fun and there's nothing I like better than playing in big games with lots of people watching. I just hope I get a chance to put on a show.'

Vini knew he would need to be patient. He was only sixteen, and his more experienced teammates would likely be the first choices for the coach, Gilmar Popoca. But that didn't stop Vini from showing off his tricks in training.

Before the first game, Coach Popoca waved Vini over for a quick chat. 'You had another excellent session today,' he said, patting Vini on the back. 'It would have been easy to go into your shell around the older players, but you faced the challenge head on.'

Vini grinned – he always did, but this time his grin was even wider.

'I'm not going to throw you straight into the action, though,' Coach Popoca explained. 'I think it's important that you get a glimpse of the Copinha first. You'll be on the bench for the first game against Central, but stay ready and we'll get you on in the second half.'

Coach Popoca paused, spotting the disappointment that had replaced the grin on Vini's face.

'Don't worry!' he added. 'You're going to make a big impact at the Copinha. I can feel it already.'

Vini nodded. Even though he wanted to play every possible second, he understood. Instead of sulking, he focused on how he would make the most of his substitute cameo – however short it might be.

With Flamengo leading 1–0 in the second half, Vini joined the other substitutes to stretch and jog down the touchline. As he re-tied his laces, he got the signal from Coach Popoca.

'It's Vini Time,' Coach Popoca said, smiling. 'You're coming on. Go out there and get on the ball.'

Vini took off his warm-up top and replaced it with his Number 18 Flamengo shirt. This was it!

He jogged onto the pitch, trying to take it all in. But there was no time to feel proud or nervous. He had a job to do, and that started with making runs to be an outlet for his teammates.

From the touchline, Vini had noticed that the Central defence wasn't the quickest. If he got even half a yard ahead of them, he would be in the clear, and he sensed the panic after his first few runs. They were scared of his pace.

A long clearance looped over his head, but he turned and sprinted after it. Two defenders hesitated and Vini poked the ball away from them. No-one was catching him now. He raced into the box and fired a low shot into the bottom corner.

Gooooooooooooooooooooooaaaaaaaaaaaaaaaaalllllllllllllll llllllllllll!!!!!!!!!!!!!!!!!!!!

Vini would never forget that feeling of seeing the net ripple. His teammates swarmed around him, wrapping him in hugs.

'You little genius!' yelled Patrick, one of the team's midfielders.

But Vini wasn't finished. The Central defence now looked even more terrified that he would skip past them with one simple turn, so his markers sat deeper and deeper. As a promising Flamengo move started down the left wing, Vini drifted over.

'Lay it inside!' he screamed, making sure Kleber, the left back, could hear him over the cheering fans.

Kleber clipped a pass right to Vini's feet. Vini instantly knew what he wanted to do. He waited for the nearest Central defender to lunge a little off-balance and then took a quick touch. That was all the space he needed to whip a curling, dipping shot into the top corner.

Goooooooooooooooooooaaaaaaaaaaaaaaaalllllllllllll lllllllllll!!!!!!!!!!!!!!!!!!

'What a hit!' Lincoln shouted. 'You're making the Copinha look easy!'

'I'm just getting started!' Vini replied, grinning as he walked back to the halfway line and giving a thumbs up to Coach Popoca on the touchline. The substitution had worked perfectly.

Now Flamengo were rolling, with Vini looking more and more at home. He could go left or right, he might take a quick shot or run through his bag of tricks first, and his speed was electric. In a matter of days, Vini had emerged as one of the team's biggest threats.

He used that pace to set up two goals in the 6–0 win over Nacional as Flamengo made it through to the knockout rounds. Vini heard the Nacional coach urging his players to press him, and he was happy to attract all that attention and then set up his teammates.

Before he knew it, Vini was preparing for the next round against Cruzeiro, and his performances had become the talk of the Copinha.

'You're one of the youngest players at the tournament, and you've been unstoppable,' Coach Popoca said. 'But stay calm out there, even if the defenders are trying to wind you up.'

As the minutes ticked by, Flamengo and Cruzeiro were locked in a 1–1 stalemate, but Vini still believed that a chance would come.

'Keep looking for that through ball!' he called to Patrick and Lucas in midfield.

Flamengo won a corner on the right, and Vini took his usual position just in front of the goalkeeper.

He wasn't likely to win many headers against taller defenders, but he was good at being in the right position if the ball bounced loose.

The corner was whipped in towards the near post and was flicked on as two players jumped for the ball. Vini reacted fastest, spinning quickly to chest the ball past the keeper and over the line.

Goooooooooooooooooooaaaaaaaaaaaaaaaalllllllllllll llllllllllll!!!!!!!!!!!!!!!!!!!!!

It was surely the winning goal. Normally Vini was cool and calm with his goal celebrations, but this one was different. He just started running – and he wasn't even sure where he was going. Luckily, his teammates were soon jumping on his back.

The dressing-room scene was joyful and loud. Music blared, the players danced and Vini was buried in more hugs.

Flamengo's Copinha run ended with a loss to Corinthians in the quarter-final, but once the pain faded, Vini had so many great memories from the 2017 Copinha. As he packed his bag to return home, he could really feel that his career was taking off.

CHAPTER 7

U17 CHAMPIONS IN CHILE

'Tomorrow, I'm going to be chilling in Chile!' Vini joked as he packed two pairs of shorts into his bag. Wesley and Luiz waited patiently. They were going to kick the ball around at the park one last time before he left.

'Don't rub it in,' Luiz said, pretending to kick Vini in the shins. 'Things are never as much fun when you're not here.'

Just a month after the Copinha, Vini was now preparing for another big tournament – the South American Under-17 Championship in Chile. But he wouldn't have the same advantage of being a surprise package this time. The world would be watching.

'How are you going to top what you did at the Copinha?' Wesley asked. 'Maybe a bicycle kick from the halfway line?'

'No, what about a penalty with your eyes closed?' Luiz added.

Vini laughed. 'I can always rely on you guys for great ideas. Honestly, I just want to put on a show – and win, of course.'

He joined his teammates for the trip to Chile and was happy to see some familiar faces. Lincoln and Alan were known to be among the next special wave of young Brazilian stars, and Paulinho was really skilful too.

Drawn in Group B, the Brazilians would face Peru, Venezuela, Paraguay and Argentina for a place in the final group stage. With expectations for Brazil always sky-high, U17 coach Carlos Amadeu warned his players about the big job ahead.

'As soon as you put on that yellow Brazil shirt, you're getting the very best from every opponent,' Coach Amadeu told his squad. 'They all want to beat Brazil. We've got a proud tradition to keep up at this tournament and, looking around this room, I'm confident we've got a great chance to lift the trophy.'

Vini grinned and gave a fist bump to Lincoln, who was sitting next to him. 'Ready to dominate?' he asked, winking.

Brazil got off to a strong start, winning three of their four group games, including a 2–0 win over rivals Argentina. Vini scored two goals during the opening group phase – and he knew he had an extra gear for the bigger games ahead.

But after a 2–2 draw with Paraguay, he sat for a long time in the dressing room, taking off his socks and shin pads much more slowly than usual. He knew he had to do more to lead the team forward.

'I can play better,' he admitted to one of the Brazil coaches. 'I'd give myself a seven out of ten so far. I want to be a ten in the Final Stage.'

Thankfully, the games kept coming and he didn't have to wait long for the next one – against Venezuela, who had been tricky opponents in the group stage.

After the warm-up, Vini felt great. 'Let's go!' he

yelled, clapping his hands as the players walked back into the dressing room. 'It's time to remind people that we're the big dogs at this tournament.'

Vini was everywhere in the first half, enjoying the freedom that Coach Amadeu had given him. Sticking on the right wing at first, he raced onto a long ball and fired a cross into the box. The Venezuela defence reacted just in time to scramble it away. Vini put his hands on his head.

'Keep finding Vini!' Coach Amadeu called, spotting the mismatch against the Venezuela left-back.

A few minutes later, Vini got another chance. Brazil swept forward and Lincoln laid the ball off to Vini just inside the penalty area. Vini took a touch, then unleashed a low shot. It bounced back off the post, rebounded off a Venezuela defender and ended up in the net. 1–0!

Goooooooooooooooooooooaaaaaaaaaaaaaaaaaalllllllllllllll llllllllllll!!!!!!!!!!!!!!!!!!!

Vini raced over to the touchline, tongue out, waving his hands. He was wrapped in hugs from the Brazil substitutes and the rest of the team followed.

Now Vini had found his extra gear. Lincoln played him through with another good pass and no-one was catching Vini. He tried a clever chip over the keeper but got it just wrong. Seconds later, Brazil doubled their lead from a corner.

'Don't relax now,' Coach Amadeu reminded his players at half-time. 'We're at our best when we're attacking.'

Vini got plenty of the ball again in the second half. His through ball set up Paulinho but his shot was well saved. Vini clapped his teammate's run.

As Venezuela pushed forward in the final ten minutes, Vini sensed more chances against a tired defence. The Brazilians intercepted a pass in midfield and the counterattack was on. Yuri Alberto curled a low shot towards the bottom corner. The Venezuela keeper tipped the ball away, but Vini reacted quickest, slotting the rebound into the net. 3–0!

Goooooooooooooooooooooaaaaaaaaaaaaaaaallllllllllllll llllllllllll!!!!!!!!!!!!!!!!!!!

Now the party could start. There was even time for Brazil to add another goal to cap off an overwhelming

4–0 win.

'That's more like it!' Vini shouted, as the Brazil players danced around the dressing room.

A win over Ecuador in the next game of the Final Stage would put Brazil in a great position – and Vini was ready to lead the charge. At the end of one training session, he saw Coach Amadeu walking slowly towards him.

'Feeling good?' Coach Amadeu asked.

'Always!' Vini replied, grinning.

'That's what I like to hear. These next few games are going to be tough, but this is where the top players really shine. You've seen it with Ronaldinho, Robinho and Neymar. I mention those names because that's how highly I think of you. Set the tone and your teammates will follow.'

Within minutes against Ecuador, Vini saw that he was going to have a fun day. After his first few runs, the Ecuador defenders were pointing to each other desperately.

Then a quick attack sent Weverson clear down the left. Vini had already drifted in from the right wing

and now he sprinted in front of his marker. He only
needed to be half a step ahead. The cross was exactly
where he wanted it and Vini squeezed a low shot
under the keeper and into the net.

*Goooooooooooooooooooaaaaaaaaaaaaaaaallllllllllllll
llllllllllll!!!!!!!!!!!!!!!!!!!!!*

With his speed, Vini knew he could get behind
the defence whenever he wanted. 'Keep looking for
my runs,' he called to Lincoln and Marcos Antônio,
signalling the kind of diagonal move he would be
making.

Minutes later, Vini passed the ball to Lincoln and
set off again. Darting in from the left wing, he left his
marker behind. Lincoln spotted him and looped the
ball over the top into Vini's path.

Vini didn't panic as the ball bounced up. He took
his time and steered the ball through the keeper's legs.

*Goooooooooooooooooooaaaaaaaaaaaaaaaallllllllllllll
llllllllllll!!!!!!!!!!!!!!!!!!!!!*

With big smiles, Vini and Lincoln danced while
the crowd cheered. Brazil were cruising now. In the

second half, Vini had a chance for his hat-trick but scuffed the shot. It bobbled to Lincoln, who stretched out his leg to tap the ball into the net.

'Even when you mis-hit the ball, it works out for you!' Lincoln shouted as they ran off to celebrate.

'We're unstoppable!' Vini called back.

Suddenly, Vini couldn't miss. In training, every shot flew past the Brazil keepers.

'It's a lot more fun when I'm watching you smashing the ball past other teams' keepers,' Gabriel Brazão called out as he picked another ball out of the net. 'Just save some of these goals for Colombia.'

That was the next test. A win here would put the U17 South American Championship trophy within reach.

Vini could see the Colombia defenders dropping deeper when he got the ball, as none of them wanted to be embarrassed by his speed. But a hopeful long ball over the top gave Vini a chance to sprint clear. It was a tough angle, but he spotted the Colombia keeper coming off his line. With his confidence higher

than ever, Vini didn't even consider taking a touch.
He just chipped the ball first-time high into the air and
over the keeper. It bounced on the line and up into
the roof of the net.

*Gooooooooooooooooooooaaaaaaaaaaaaaaaalllllllllllllll
llllllllllllll!!!!!!!!!!!!!!!!!!!!!*

The dancing was back! Lincoln and Alan joined
Vini. Gabriel was standing outside his box, clapping
and smiling. 'See!' he called. 'It's much better when I
get to watch you scoring against other keepers!'

'To have the confidence to take that shot is one
thing,' Coach Amadeu told him at half-time as
they walked back to the dressing room. 'Scoring so
effortlessly is just incredible.'

In the second half, Vini continued to find space
on the left. Alan knocked a pass behind the defence
and there was only ever going to be one winner in
that race. Vini sprinted on, took a quick look to see
where the keeper was and fired in a low shot. The net
rippled again.

Gooooooooooooooooooooaaaaaaaaaaaaaaaalllllllllllllll

///////////////!!!!!!!!!!!!!!!!!!!!!!

'What a pass!' he shouted as Alan ran over.

'Magic finish too!' Alan said as they looked for the nearest camera to strike a pose.

As the last game loomed, Brazil still needed at least a draw against Chile to clinch the trophy. A talented Chile team had recorded three 1–0 wins in the Final Stage, but facing Vini in this kind of form would be a whole different challenge.

Vini quickly saw that Chile's game plan was centred on him, with two defenders shadowing him. During a short injury stoppage, Vini was near the touchline and Coach Amadeu waved him over. 'If they want to give you all that attention, that's fine,' he said. 'It just gives our other boys more space to play. When you get on the ball, move it quickly to Alan and Lincoln so we can catch the defence out of position.'

That's exactly what he did – and Chile were soon in trouble. Lincoln found Paulinho for the first goal, then Alan curled in a brilliant free kick. As Brazil piled on three more goals, the jumping and dancing began on the touchline. Vini went close with a curling shot off the outside of his foot, but he had to settle for a total of seven goals at the tournament. It was enough for him to finish as the U17 South American Championship top scorer.

Sometimes Vini had to pinch himself to believe the first few months of 2017. He had just taken on the best young players in South American football – and he had outshone them all! Clutching the Championship trophy in one hand and his Best Player award in the other, Vini smiled his trademark smile and stood patiently for photos.

CHAPTER 8

ROBINHO VS. THE NEW ROBINHO

Back at Flamengo, Vini was clearly on the first team fast track. He felt ready and the fans were desperate to see him on the pitch. But there was never any danger of Vini thinking he was suddenly a big deal. Uncle Ulysses and Auntie Tatiana were always there to keep his feet on the ground.

'What are we meant to call you these days?' Auntie Tatiana asked at breakfast, teasing him. 'Is it The New Neymar or The New Robinho?'

Vini rolled his eyes. 'Don't you start with that too! I'm just Vini.'

'Oh, good,' she replied. 'Because I know Vini and I trust him to wash the plates well.' She put the sponge in his hand and laughed.

Ever since his Copinha highlights and the special run with the Brazil Under-17s, Vini had been dealing with a lot more attention. There was always a search for the next big thing in Brazilian football – and he was proud that his name was part of that conversation. But he still had a long way to go.

With dazzling performances in training, Vini was soon winning over Flamengo manager Zé Ricardo. Day after day, he was the star of the 5-a-side games.

'Beautiful, Vini!' Zé Ricardo called after one clever turn that wrong-footed his marker.

As Vini jogged back, he heard another coach standing next to Zé Ricardo. 'I can't wait to see what that boy can do in a real game,' he said.

'He'll get his chance soon,' Zé Ricardo said. 'He's running rings round our defenders.'

That just gave Vini even more confidence. He called for a pass and controlled the ball instantly with his left foot. As he dribbled forward, the nearest player hesitated. Vini had a reputation for leaving defenders on the ground in training with a change of direction or a quick stepover. This time, he rolled the ball from foot to foot, then nutmegged the defender.

The move was met with 'Oooh' and 'Whoa!' from his teammates. Even Zé Ricardo had a little smile on his face.

The next day, Zé Ricardo called Vini to the touchline during one of the morning drills. Vini took a deep breath, hoping this was going to be good news.

'You can probably guess what this is about!' Zé Ricardo said, grinning.

Vini didn't know what to say, so he just grinned too.

'You're one of the most talented kids I've seen in all my years of coaching,' Zé Ricardo continued. 'We've been cautious not to throw too much at you until you're ready – but you've earned this. You'll be in the squad to play Atlético Mineiro this weekend. We'll start you on the bench, but I'm hoping to get you some minutes.'

Vini woke early on the morning of the game and had already finished his breakfast when Auntie Tatiana appeared, clearly hiding something behind her back.

He raised an eyebrow, wondering what this was all

about.

'Do you remember this?' she asked, holding out a folded piece of paper.

Vini took it and opened it. He laughed. Of course he remembered.

It was a picture of Robinho, cut out from a local newspaper, that had been on Vini's bedroom wall for years. Back then, Robinho had become his idol – and he had been a huge fan ever since. Vini loved the way he ran with the ball and wasn't afraid to try his tricks in any situation.

Vini thought back to his playground days, when he and his friends were pretending to be Brazil stars. He always had to be Robinho.

Now Robinho was playing for Atlético Mineiro.

'I thought this was a good moment to show you this and remind you how far you've come,' Auntie Tatiana added, winking. 'Plus, you might see him today!'

Vini grinned. 'I hope so!'

When he got to the stadium, Vini just tried to follow what the other Flamengo players were doing so he didn't look silly for not knowing how things

worked on a match day. He took his place on the
bench with the other substitutes and, feeling both
excited and nervous, he was glad to get up to jog and
stretch on the touchline after twenty minutes.

Vini waited patiently for his chance, and he kept
one eye on the scoreboard. The minutes were ticking
by.

With less than ten minutes to go, Zé Ricardo looked
across to his substitutes standing nearby and waved
Vini over. One of the assistant coaches was making
the substitution sign. Vini froze for a second, as if he
couldn't move his arms and legs, and then hurried
over. He was about to make his professional debut.

'Good luck out there,' Zé Ricardo said, shaking
Vini's hand and putting an arm round his shoulders as
they waited for the ball to go out of play. 'Take them
on when you get the chance. Their defenders will be
tired and we'll get some chances to counterattack.'

Running onto the pitch, Vini couldn't help but
glance towards the other end, where Robinho was
standing. He was on the same pitch as one of his
biggest childhood heroes!

Vini only got a few touches in the short time he was on the pitch, but it was an unforgettable highlight. He tried to soak it all in – the fans, the pitch, the speed of the game.

After the final whistle, everything was a blur for Vini except his handshake with Robinho. That was a moment he would replay in his head over and over again.

'I'm just starting out with Flamengo, but you've been a big inspiration for me,' Vini said, as they shook hands. His voice sounded shaky.

Robinho smiled. 'That's always great to hear,' he said. 'I'm down to my last few years now, but I love knowing that I've had an impact on the next wave of Brazilian players.'

'Any advice on how I can get to the next level?' Vini asked.

'Keep working hard – in training, in the gym, but never lose the style in your game. I could see straight away that you were a showman! That's what football is all about.'

Vini glided off the pitch, feeling like life couldn't get much better than this.

CHAPTER 9

THE REAL DEAL

Vini did his best to focus on his football, but it was impossible to ignore some of the rumours linking him with big-money transfers to a top European league. His youth team performances for Flamengo and Brazil had got the scouts' attention – but which club would come forward with the winning offer?

Thousands of miles away in Madrid, Vini was a hot topic. The Real Madrid directors had gathered to discuss possible transfer deals – and it didn't take long for his name to come up.

'We've been watching Vinícius Jr. for months and our sense is that Flamengo would be willing to listen to offers,' one of the head scouts explained.

'Look, we all remember what happened with Neymar,' another voice added, wincing as he said it.

There were silent nods around the table. Real had lost out to Barcelona in the race for Neymar – and that one still hurt.

'We gave that our best shot, but then added more resources and expanded our scouting network – all for exactly this moment. So we can't hesitate on this one. We've got to move now.'

'I'd be shocked if he wasn't on Barcelona's radar too. Imagine the fans' reaction if they beat us to another big deal!'

'But let's remember that he's sixteen and he's played less than twenty minutes of first team football,' another voice added. 'It's easy to see the potential – I just wonder if we've seen enough to take a big swing here.'

'Right, and that's the risk. If we wait for him to gain a bit more experience and a more polished end product, we'll be battling every top club in Europe for his signature – and probably paying double the price.'

Florentino Pérez sighed as all eyes turned to him. 'I

think we know what we've got to do,' he said. 'Let's make this happen.'

Sure enough, Barcelona were interested too and wanted to bring Vini to the Nou Camp. The battle had begun – and all Vini could do was wait.

As Vini lay in bed one night, staring at the ceiling, his phone buzzed. He stretched over to his bedside table and checked the screen. It was his agent. He got out of bed, turned on the light and answered it.

'Sorry to call so late,' a cheery voice said, barely pausing to catch his breath. 'Look, I know we've talked about the different clubs that might be interested in you and how you can't let that distract you, but I couldn't keep this one to myself. I'm hearing that Flamengo are in talks with Real Madrid about signing you.'

Vini felt his legs turn to jelly as he stumbled over to the nearest chair. 'Really?!!'

'Would I joke about something this important?' his agent replied, laughing.

'Well… erm… I guess not…' Vini replied. 'This is wild! It's all happening so fast! Call me back if you hear anything else – there's no way I'll be sleeping now!'

The deal was done the next day, with Real Madrid paying £38 million. Vini almost fell over when he heard that transfer fee! But he didn't have to say his goodbyes just yet. With this deal, he would stay at Flamengo until he turned eighteen, before making Madrid his new home.

Before the announcement, Vini walked his family through all the twists and turns of the past few weeks.

'It's just a bit of a strange feeling,' Vini admitted as he joined his parents for lunch. 'I've signed for Real Madrid but I'm still a Flamengo player and yet everyone knows that I'm only here for another year.'

'Yeah, what a roller-coaster ride!' Fernanda said. 'It's only natural to feel unsettled by all of this. Just take it one day at a time.'

Vini nodded. 'For now, I'm just going to focus on Flamengo,' he said. 'I want to finish in good form and leave behind some special memories for the fans.'

In some ways, the pressure was off Vini's shoulders. There would be no more rumours about possible transfers and fewer scouts popping up in the crowd.

Despite all the excitement around the move to Real Madrid, it was easy to forget that Vini was still a teenager finding his way in the Flamengo first team. He was playing well in training and learning as much as he could from the older players on how to prepare for games and look after his body. Sometimes Vini was surprised at how willing the Flamengo defenders were to help him after some of the tricks he had pulled off against them in training.

The coaches loved having Vini as a super sub. In that role, he could come on in the second half and make a big impact, terrifying tired defenders with his endless running. But he was still searching for his first goal.

'I haven't had many chances so far, but I'm going to keep making my runs and getting into good positions,' he told his parents before a Copa Sudamericana game against Palestino. 'I just really want to have the feeling of celebrating with the fans.'

'Be patient and stay calm,' his dad reminded him. 'That first goal is coming, and we can't wait to see it!'

'I've already thought of a few goal celebrations,' Vini added. 'But in the moment, I'm sure I'll forget them and just run around like a little kid in the park!'

By now, Vini had a routine as a substitute. He knew how much running and stretching he needed to do to stay ready, and how much water to drink before coming on. As long as he got that right, he could make an instant impact.

With the Palestino game under control, Vini got the 'you're coming on' signal from one of the coaches. There were twenty minutes to go and he had already spotted a few Palestino defenders who looked exhausted. He jumped on the spot and checked his studs before running on.

It didn't take long for a chance to arrive. A long Flamengo clearance set Vini free down the left wing and he sprinted ahead. Though his first thought was to shoot, he looked up and saw a red-and-black shirt at the back post.

Unselfishly, Vini chose to go for the assist. The cross was almost perfect, but a defender jumped at the last minute and the ball rebounded back across the penalty area.

Vini's eyes lit up. It was coming straight back to him. Some players might have taken a touch just to avoid the risk of a bad bounce, but Vini didn't hesitate. He smashed a first-time shot past the goalkeeper.

Goooooooooooooooooooaaaaaaaaaaaaaaaallllllllllllll llllllllllll!!!!!!!!!!!!!!!!!!!!!

What a moment! His first goal for the Flamengo first team! His heart was pounding as he sprinted over to the touchline, where he was wrapped in hugs from the substitutes and coaches. The other players rushed over to join him.

At the final whistle, Vini ran over to get the match ball from the referee and tucked it safely under his arm. He wanted that for his collection.

'I'm going to remember today forever,' he told his parents that night, unpacking a box of things from the game and holding up his shirt. 'I might never wash this!'

'Gross!' his mum replied, making a face – and they both fell onto the sofa laughing.

CHAPTER 10

THE COPA GUANABARA

Vini had a taste for trophies after his Under-17 success with Brazil, and he was determined to win something for Flamengo before his move to Real Madrid.

The Copa Guanabara was one path to a trophy. Flamengo had made it to the last four, but their chances of lifting the Copa Guanabara depended on getting past Botafogo, another club from Rio de Janeiro.

'They'll be desperate to beat us,' Vini's teammates explained. 'We've got more talent than them, but we've got to match their energy.'

As Vini warmed up, the Botafogo fans didn't exactly give him a warm welcome. But he was expecting that after all the attention around his big transfer. It only took a few minutes for the harsh words to start.

'Hey, try staying on your feet instead of rolling around on the floor!'

'Crybaby! Crybaby!'

Vini had an endless number of bumps and bruises on his shins and ankles from rough tackles, but it would never stop him from doing his tricks and trying to embarrass defenders. Often, though, he had a painful walk back to the dressing room after games.

Did he sometimes go for one extra roll to make sure the referee gave a free kick? Sure, but nothing worse than that.

Still, the fans had clearly made up their minds from watching Vini this season that he was faking, diving, trying to get defenders booked, or some combination of the three. He heard the chants but blocked them out as he stretched near the corner flag.

If anything, the crowd chanted and whistled louder when they saw Vini coming on in the second half. 'Crybaby! Crybaby!'

Vini grinned. 'We'll see,' he muttered to himself.

Flamengo attacked down the left wing. Moments later, the ball found its way to Vini on the edge of the box. He only had one thought in his mind: shoot.

He got his defender off balance with a little dip of the shoulder, shifted the ball slightly and then curled an unstoppable shot over the keeper's outstretched arm and into the top corner.

Goooooooooooooooooooaaaaaaaaaaaaaaaaaalllllllllllllll lllllllllll!!!!!!!!!!!!!!!!!!!!

Vini took a second to admire the perfect strike, then he spun away to celebrate. With all the emotions pumping through his body, he was fired up – and he hadn't forgotten the chants from the Botafogo fans.

Before any of his teammates could talk him out of it, Vini turned to the crowd and started making a crying gesture to the fans. 'Who's crying now?' he thought.

To his surprise, his goal celebration seemed to get as much attention as the big story of Flamengo reaching the Copa Guanabara. It was his way at hitting back at the fans – and he was just having fun with it.

Even so, it was a good lesson for Vini. He knew that there were moments when he lost his temper on the pitch – and this wouldn't be the last time when he had to be reminded to stay calm in these high-pressure moments. Of course opponents were going to try to rattle him – Vini had to be prepared for that kind of response when he was busy trying to make defenders look silly with his quick feet, stepovers and shimmies.

'Never let them see that they're getting to you, even if they are,' warned Juan, one of the most experienced Flamengo players. 'A defender could be yelling at you all game, kicking you off the ball or pulling your shirt, but you'll be the one sent off if you lose your cool.'

In the meantime, Vini had to prepare for the Copa Guanabara against Boavista. He was again named among the substitutes but, like against Botafogo, he hoped to make a big impact when it was time for fresh legs and a creative spark. The change came with thirty minutes to go, and Vini did a couple of final stretches as he waited on the touchline.

'Give us an outlet,' the coaches said, clapping excitedly. 'Look for the long diagonal ball over the top.'

Vini felt sharp from his very first touch. Flamengo were 1–0 up, but it was a dangerous lead. One more goal would make the last ten minutes much calmer.

Éverton Ribeiro got the ball thirty yards out. Instead of taking a shot, he dinked an inviting pass into the box. Vini had guessed what was coming and he got there so fast that it seemed like he was surely offside. But he wasn't. He got the slightest of touches on the pass, helping the ball into the bottom corner.

Gooooooooooooooooooooaaaaaaaaaaaaaaaalllllllllllllll llllllllll!!!!!!!!!!!!!!!!!!!

Game over! Vini jogged over to the fans with his arm in the air and a big smile on his face. Flamengo would soon be lifting the Copa Guanabara trophy.

There were shouts and screams of excitement at the final whistle, and Vini went from teammate to teammate, hugging and dancing.

This was exactly why he had been so happy to stay at Flamengo just a little longer – the chance to continue the bonds that he had built with his teammates and chase a trophy together. Job done!

CHAPTER 11

REAL TEARS THIS TIME

'Leaving is going to be even harder than I expected,' Vini told Wesley and Luiz as they packed a few more of his things into bags and boxes ready for Madrid. There was still so much to do.

That afternoon, Flamengo were playing Paraná – and it would be Vini's last game for the club before joining Real Madrid. The months had really flown by since the announcement of his move and it was all becoming very real, very fast.

His contacts at Real were doing their best to make his life easier, from arranging where he would stay with his family when he first arrived, to making sure his training kit would be waiting for him.

Throughout this whole process, Vini had been so impressed with all of Real's efforts. Before agreeing to sign with the club, he and his family had visited the Bernabéu and met some of the players. Back then, Real had promised to support him – and they had certainly kept their word.

Any time he saw highlights of a La Liga game, Vini's head was filled with thoughts about what it would be like to play at the Bernabéu against some of the world's biggest teams. He loved the way the teams played, with so much dribbling and trickery. Even the defenders had skills!

'Alright, enough daydreaming, big man,' Luiz called, throwing a T-shirt for Vini to put in his bag.

Vini snapped back to the present and took a deep breath. He looked around the room. He was ready for the challenge of a new start in Spain, but it would take some time to adjust to life away from Brazil.

First, though, he had a game to win, and he was determined to put on one last show for the Flamengo fans. He wanted to finish with a win.

The crowd knew the significance of this game, and

they were chanting Vini's name from the minute he stepped onto the pitch with his teammates. He looked at the stands filled with red-and-black shirts, and waved and blew kisses to the fans.

It wasn't his best game, but how could it be with all the emotions floating around? Though he made his usual runs and was just as adventurous as ever with his silky footwork, nothing quite clicked. But the fans didn't seem to care. They still cheered every touch and sang his name as loudly as they could.

Flamengo won 2–0, but Vini couldn't even think about that score after the game. When a local TV channel appeared with a microphone, and asked how he was feeling, he couldn't hold back the tears any longer. He sobbed as he tried to find the right words to answer the questions.

'This club has given me everything,' Vini explained, finally. 'It's a real family. Football gave me a path to a better life, but I could never have got this far without all the great people at Flamengo. I'll never forget all the special memories here.'

He clapped to the fans and hugged his teammates.

It was the end of one chapter in his life and the start of an exciting new one.

Later that week, Vini and his agent looked through the final plans for Madrid, including the cool villa where Vini and his family would be living.

Luckily, after the long, tearful goodbyes with the Flamengo fans, Vini was bringing lots of people with him to Spain. His parents and his aunt and uncle would be making the trip. Wesley and Luiz would be there too. Vini couldn't wait to share this adventure with all of them.

CHAPTER 12

A SPECIAL WELCOME IN MADRID

'Vinícius! Vini! Welcome to Madrid!'

'We love you!!!!'

There was no escaping the screams from the fans who were crammed into one corner of the Bernabéu for Vini's official unveiling as a Real Madrid player. He smiled and waved. This was a day he had been dreaming about for a long time – basically ever since the deal was agreed to join the Spanish giants.

The club's directors were pulling out all the stops to make this a memorable introduction to life at Real Madrid. So far, Vini was loving every second of it. Wearing the crisp white Real shirt, he kissed the badge and kept the big smile plastered on his face.

Out of nowhere, a ball appeared on the pitch. As photographers circled around him, Vini began to juggle the ball, letting it drop onto his shoulder, then back to his feet. The Bernabéu pitch felt like a big green carpet – and, for today, it was all his.

As he turned to face the nearest photographer, Vini caught sight of movement from the Real dugout. He turned to the nearest Real Madrid rep. 'Wait, is… is that, erm…?'

Vini looked again. Yes! It was Ronaldo! He hadn't felt too nervous about meeting all the Real fans, but suddenly his legs were shaking. Ronaldo was here! Wow!!

'From one Brazilian to another, I'm here to welcome you to this incredible club,' Ronaldo said, shaking Vini's hand. 'You're going to have an amazing career at Real.'

Vini was speechless. He just nodded and smiled, then finally managed to add: 'Thanks so much. This is all unbelievable!'

Ronaldo was such a legend in Brazil. Vini's family still talked about his magic performances at the 2002

World Cup that led Brazil to glory, and he had won the league twice at Real Madrid. Now he was here at the Bernabéu to welcome Vini to the club.

Just when Vini didn't think this day could get any more special, it was time to take some photos on the pitch with his family.

With tears in their eyes, his parents joined him on the pitch. They looked up at the huge stadium – the fancy seats, the big screens, the perfectly cut grass. They watched in stunned silence as their son, who was really still a kid, waved to his new fans.

Vini jogged over, still dribbling the ball from foot to foot. His parents wrapped him in hugs and didn't want to let go. 'Congratulations, son!' his dad said. 'This is a dream come true to be here with you!'

Vini smiled. He was thinking about what it would be like to play a game in this stadium. It was already giving him goosebumps – and that was before they packed 80,000 cheering fans inside.

'I had the chance to choose between the top teams in the world and I went for the best of them all,' Vini told the reporters gathered for the presentation.

'You're destined to become one of the game's all-time greats,' Florentino said in his speech. 'Welcome to your new home.'

If this first day at Real was a sign of what life would be like in Madrid, Vini couldn't wait to get started.

CHAPTER 13

CASTILLA SCREAMERS

As Vini settled into life at Real Madrid during 2018, his big-money price tag didn't worry him too much. He believed in himself, and he was more excited than nervous about the challenge ahead.

Still, every time he arrived at the Bernabéu or the club's training complex, there was a special feeling. He had joined one of the world's best teams, packed with superstars who had won all the big trophies. Vini had a lot to live up to, but he would be able to learn from his teammates as he tried to reach their level.

The warm welcome for Vini at Real continued well beyond his unveiling in the summer, including a hug from Cristiano Ronaldo, who was still one of Vini's biggest idols. It helped to have other Brazilians in the squad too, and Marcelo and Casemiro showed Vini around the stadium, the training ground and the rest of the city. Learning the language was one of the first steps.

'How are those Spanish lessons going?' Marcelo asked as they sat in the club cafeteria after training.

'I'm getting better,' Vini replied in Spanish with a grin.

Marcelo laughed, patting his friend on the shoulder. 'Excellent! You'll be fluent in no time. But remember, I'm here if you need me.'

By now, Marcelo had learned to spot the confusion on Vini's face when he didn't understand something that manager Julen Lopetegui or one of his teammates had said. During one preseason meeting, Marcelo tapped Vini on the arm and pointed to a sheet of paper in his hand. On it, he had written a few sentences in Portuguese so that Vini understood the instructions.

'Thank you!' Vini whispered, giving Marcelo a thumbs up.

But as the La Liga season kicked off in Spain, Vini knew that he had a lot of watching and learning ahead. Real had so many attacking options. Would his progress be stalled if he sat on the bench for too long?

Vini just wanted to be on the pitch. He talked to his parents and to Marcelo. Then he reached a decision and went to talk to Julen after training.

'Could I spend some time with the Castilla team?' he asked. 'I think it'll really help me to play regularly.'

Julen looked surprised at first, but he understood. He spoke with his coaches and with Castilla boss Santi Solari. In the end, they agreed it was a good idea. Vini would still spend time around the first team, but working with Castilla could speed up his adjustment to Spanish football.

'It says a lot about you that you're excited to be with Castilla,' Solari said before Vini's first training session. 'It would have been easy for you to think you're too good for this.'

'I just want to keep getting better,' Vini replied. 'I've learned so much already from being around Cristiano, Luka, Marcelo, Sergio and all the other first-team players. But I'm at my happiest when I'm on the pitch with the ball at my feet.'

With his big smile and funny jokes, Vini fitted in with the young Castilla group instantly. He didn't walk around as if he was this big first-team star. He was just one of the boys.

In fact, he had a lot in common with the other young players. Solari had done quick introductions on his first day, and Vini spent a lot of time with Federico Valverde, another young player who was so close to his dream of playing for Real.

'Looking forward to ripping through defences together,' Federico said, giving Vini a fist bump. 'Not just with Castilla, but with Real one day too!'

Unlike most clubs, Castilla didn't play in a league with other reserve teams or academies. They were part of the Spanish third division. That meant Vini was thrown into physical battles against experienced men.

Ahead of his Castilla debut against Atlético B, Vini was full of energy. He had planned to rest the night before the game, but he was in no mood to sit quietly and watch TV. He was soon dribbling a ball around and doing whatever he could to calm his excitement.

The next morning, he met his Castilla teammates to take the bus. It was a different experience from his glimpses of life in the Real first team. There was definitely less glamour, but Vini only cared about getting to play.

He wasted no time in announcing himself with Castilla. Early on, he saw a move developing down the left and burst away from his marker. 'Yes! Yes! Play it through!'

The pass arrived and Vini took it smoothly in his stride. He shifted the ball onto his right foot and pinged a shot into the net.

Gooooooooooooooooooooaaaaaaaaaaaaaaaaalllllllllllllllllllllllllllll!!!!!!!!!!!!!!!!!!!!!!!

Now the pressure was totally off his shoulders, but he was still looking to create chances. Vini dropped deeper on the left wing to collect a pass from midfield. He cut inside with three defenders chasing him, but he already had the yard of space he needed. With no hesitation, he unleashed a thumping shot that flew past the Atlético B keeper and into the top corner.

*Goooooooooooooooooooooaaaaaaaaaaaaaaaaalllllllllllllll
lllllllllllll!!!!!!!!!!!!!!!!!!!!!*

He raced over to the touchline to celebrate with the Castilla substitutes and coaches. Even Solari joined in, reaching into the pile of players to give Vini a pat on the head.

'What a strike!!!' Federico called. 'If the keeper had got a hand on it, he'd have ended up in the net too!'

This was exactly the kind of game that Vini needed, and he felt good about his decision to push for some Castilla game time. He knew there would be plenty of Real Madrid people keeping an eye on him here anyway – and Solari had promised to give Julen regular updates.

'Great goals today, Vini,' Marcelo told him when they spoke that night. 'You're going to score for fun with Castilla and you'll be back with the first team in no time. We need you!'

Vini was on target again in the next game against Unionistas, curling a perfectly placed free kick around the wall and into the bottom corner. Opponents were quickly getting fed up of seeing Vini's Number 11 shirt flying past them.

Meanwhile, Real Madrid's 2018–19 season was already going off the rails. Things hadn't clicked with Julen and he was sacked in October 2018. While the club searched for a new boss, Solari was asked to step in.

Solari called Vini to his office the next day. 'As you've probably heard, I'm going to be working with the first team,' he said.

'I'll miss you,' Vini said, with a disappointed look.

'Well, actually you won't,' Solari explained. 'That's what I wanted to talk to you about. I've had a front row seat to see your talent over the past few weeks, and that's exactly the spark that Real need at the moment. I want you to come with me and rejoin the first team. Trust me, you won't just be stuck on the bench.'

Vini grinned. 'Sounds like a plan, boss.'

CHAPTER 14

SOARING WITH SOLARI

'Welcome back, wizard!' Marcelo said, hugging Vini as they walked over to the Real training pitch.

It was good to be back with the first team, especially with Solari's familiar face running the sessions. But there was nothing good about Real's league position. Vini had made a very brief debut against Atlético Madrid in September 2018, but now a much bigger role seemed to be opening up for him.

'The crowd are desperate for some magic and something to get excited about,' Solari reminded Vini. 'We need to make the Bernabéu electric again. This club has such a tradition of entertainers and I was lucky enough to play with Raul, Zidane and Figo.

You're already starting to remind me of some of the greats on that team.'

Solari gave Vini his full debut in late October 2018 as Real faced Melilla in the Copa del Rey. Vini tried to play it cool when he heard the news, but he was soon able to escape to a quiet corridor, where he let out a silent scream of delight.

The fans roared every time Vini got the ball, sensing that they might see a series of stepovers or another piece of skill as he attacked down the left. It was special to be out there with Federico too and they were soon linking up on quick counterattacks.

The young Real Madrid players were loving this opportunity, and Vini was involved in all the best moves. He was mainly playing on the left, but he looked to make diagonal runs when space opened up. After one quick dribble, he fired a quick shot and had his hands on his head as the keeper made a diving save.

Marco Asensio gave Real the lead, and then Vini set him up for a second goal with a mazy dribble on the left. His cutback was perfect. 'You made it easy for me!' Marco called as they celebrated with the fans.

Vini could feel the frustration from the Melilla defenders. One of them tripped him up as he sprinted clear, but Vini just bounced up and got the ball for the free kick. He fizzed another shot just wide and looked up at the sky. So close!

After another near miss, Vini set off dribbling again. He weaved left and right to keep the defenders guessing, got a few lucky bounces, then stretched to fire a low shot. The keeper saved it, but the rebound came straight back to Vini and he clipped the ball over the line.

Gooooooooooooooooooooaaaaaaaaaaaaaaaaalllllllllllllll llllllllllll!!!!!!!!!!!!!!!!!!!

He danced his way over to the fans and kissed the Real badge. His first goal for the club!

That performance against Melilla gave Vini extra confidence in training. He had heard the stories that Solari only played the young players in that game because it was the cup and Real had a big first leg lead, but Vini really believed that he belonged in the first team.

Solari did too. Vini was back on the scoresheet again at the Bernabéu against Real Valladolid, finding himself in the right place at the right time when the ball pinged around in the box. He kept his cool and poked the ball into the bottom corner.

'Let's go!!!' he yelled, as Marco and Marcelo ran over to him.

When Vini arrived home at his villa that night, everyone else was asleep. But he wasn't sleepy. He was still too fired up, so he sat down at the kitchen table with a glass of water and shook his head, grinning as he replayed his goal in his head.

'We're delivering the best show in town,' he said to himself quietly. 'This is exactly where I'm meant to be.'

CHAPTER 15

AN INJURY SETBACK

'The Champions League knockout rounds are a whole different beast,' Sergio Ramos explained to Vini as they finished the second lap of their warmup run. 'When you play the same team twice within a few weeks, it's a real battle.'

It wasn't enough to wipe the smile off Vini's face, though. He was loving life on the big stage in his first Real season – and the Champions League nights at the Bernabéu were even more special.

The Champions League draw had paired Real Madrid with Ajax, two teams with rich histories in the competition. Despite playing regularly, Vini felt fresh as he prepared for the first leg in Holland.

'They'll be terrified of your pace,' Solari told him. 'Run at their full-backs and look for Karim when you get half a yard to swing in a cross.'

It didn't take long for Vini to test the Ajax keeper. Darting inside with one of his trademark runs, he had defenders stumbling backwards and trying not to concede a penalty. He fired a shot towards the top corner, but the goalkeeper tipped the ball over the bar.

The Real threat kept coming down the left wing – Vini turned his marker inside out. One minute, he was dropping short, the next he was spinning in behind. A clipped pass down the line sent Vini on another sprint. He left one Ajax defender on the ground as he burst forward. Now two more defenders were charging across. Vini took a couple more touches to get away from them, then laid the ball off to Karim, who drilled an unstoppable shot into the net. What a move!

After an end-to-end second half, the first leg finished 2–1 to Real Madrid. Vini high-fived Luka and Marcelo. They were in a great position ahead of the return game at the Bernabéu.

Vini waited impatiently for the second leg. He loved La Liga games but there was something even more special about hearing the Champions League anthem and taking on the best teams in Europe.

There was buzz around the Bernabéu even an hour before kick-off. Vini went through his usual warm-up, with the fans starting to fill the stands.

'You gave their defenders nightmares in the first leg,' Luka said as they passed the ball around near the halfway line. 'Give us more of the same tonight. I'll be looking for your runs in behind.'

But this quickly turned into Ajax's night as they scored two quick goals. Vini could see that even some of his more experienced teammates were in shock, but there was plenty of time to fight back. Vini dropped deeper to get on the ball and then produced a mazy run that sent the Ajax defence scrambling to recover.

As he launched into a full sprint, he got into shooting range with a defender sliding in for the block. Vini was fast enough to whack a shot just wide of the post, but the defender's slide knocked him off balance and he fell awkwardly.

'Arghhhhhh!!' Vini screamed, grabbing his knee. He had dealt with lots of bumps and bruises over the years, but this was another level of pain. Vini stayed down just off the pitch as the Real physio raced over.

Vini pointed to his knee and tried to explain what the injury felt like. With his hands over his face to hide the tears, he needed some help to limp back to the dressing room.

As he sat at his locker, he stared at the floor. Now what? Probably some tests and then physio appointments and exercises. The physio and club doctor appeared and provided all the support they could – but Vini's mind was still on the game. He watched from the dressing room as Real slipped to a 4–1 loss. They were out of the Champions League.

But, while his teammates had the chance to make amends in La Liga, Vini could only watch as life at Real Madrid went on without him. The test results confirmed ruptured ligaments in his knee – so surgery and rest lay ahead. He wouldn't be able to play, or even kick a ball, for months.

It was a tough way to end such an exciting first season in Madrid, but Vini had been happy with his progress and the bond he was building with the Real fans. Vini's absence hit the Real players hard too, with so many of the team's best attacks featuring his wizardry.

Worst of all, Vini could do nothing to help Solari dig his way out of a poor run of results. As Real continued to wobble, Solari was sacked.

But Vini just tried to focus on what he could control. With his friends and family cheering him on, he gave every last bit of energy to his recovery – in the gym, working on exercises, teaming up with the club physios.

'I'm going to come back better and stronger than ever,' he told Marcelo as he finished another set of exercises. 'Spread the word!'

CHAPTER 16

BRAZIL BREAKTHROUGH

The long hours of treatment and exercises finally got Vini fit enough to rejoin the Real training sessions. His knee felt strong, and he was ready to make up for lost time. But there were more twists and turns ahead on his journey back to full fitness. For a start, Zidane had returned for a second spell as Real manager, and Vini would have to prove himself again.

'I wish I hadn't missed the end of last season,' he said to Casemiro one afternoon. 'I feel like I'm way down the pecking order with Zidane.'

It was true that Real had an embarrassment of riches for the attacking roles in Zidane's 4-3-3 formation. Vini was willing to be patient and play the super sub role when needed, but there were no guarantees there either.

Vini knew he had areas of his game to work on, like his finishing. Zidane had talked to him about that a few times, urging him to work on a more consistent end product, whether that was crossing or shooting. Too often, he would rush and waste a good opening.

Even so, his talent was clear, and Vini was on the radar for the Brazil squad.

'So, when are we going to see you in a Brazil shirt for your international debut?' his dad asked during their weekly talk.

'Well, I got a call-up just before my knee injury, so I know I'm in their plans,' Vini answered. 'Hopefully I won't have to wait much longer.'

Sure enough, ahead of the September 2019 international break, Vinícius got the news he was hoping for, with a surprise phone call from Brazil manager Tite.

'Congratulations, Vini,' Tite said. 'We know you're going to be a big part of the Brazil team for many years to come. The friendly against Peru will be a great chance for you to experience the set-up and spend time with the other players.'

'Thanks, Coach,' Vini replied. 'I was so sad to miss it last time. I'll be ready to make up for lost time.'

As soon as the Brazil squad was announced, the messages came pouring in, wishing Vini good luck. Everyone promised to be watching. Vini just hoped to get a few minutes on the pitch.

Even being part of the Brazil training sessions felt like a treat. Vini was on the same team as Neymar for some of the drills and he tried not to look too star-struck.

On game day, he listened carefully to all the instructions and then watched eagerly from the bench. As the minutes ticked by in the second half, Vini started to wonder whether he would get a chance to play. It was a tight game and there were so many other talented players for Tite to call on.

But with about twenty minutes to go, one of the Brazil coaches turned to Vini on the bench. 'Get yourself loose,' he said. 'You'll be coming on in a few minutes.'

Vini hopped out of his seat and bounced down the touchline. The thought of his family and friends gathered around a TV back in Brazil sent a shiver down his back. This moment was going to be for them as well as for him.

The ball went out for a throw-in and the referee blew his whistle so that Brazil could make the substitution. Vini rearranged his shin pads one last time and waited for Richarlison to jog off.

'Good luck, young gun,' Richarlison said, high-fiving him and patting him on the back.

The rest of the game felt like a blur. Vini was so focused on making the right runs and showing a sharp first touch that it was only after the game that it really sank in that he had been sharing the pitch with Neymar, Philippe Coutinho and other Brazil stars. But after two solid days in training with the squad, Vini was no longer in awe – he felt like he belonged on this stage.

Looking down at his yellow Brazil shirt as he walked off the pitch, Vini had never felt so proud. Yes, he had represented his country at youth levels and enjoyed lots of great moments. But this was different. This was the Brazil team that he had always dreamed of playing in.

Vini knew that the next job was helping to end Brazil's World Cup drought. The team had last gone all the way to winning the tournament in 2002, but had stumbled through some disappointing performances since then. The recent Copa América success had raised expectations again, but there was still a lot of work ahead.

'That's the first of many caps, I'm sure,' Tite said, hugging Vini on the touchline after the final whistle. 'I can't wait to see what you'll do in the years ahead.'

'We're going to put Brazil back on top!' Vini replied, grinning. He was officially an international footballer now – and he would be riding this wave for as long as he could.

CHAPTER 17

EL CLÁSICO RECORD-BREAKER

'It's El Clásico week, baby!' Vini called out, laughing as he put on his boots for training. The 2019–20 season was in full flow, and he was doing his best to make the most of every first-team appearance.

'We've got to win this one,' Luka replied. 'Barcelona have embarrassed us the past few years.'

'Five years, to be exact,' Sergio added. 'Well, that's how long it's been since we beat Barça at the Bernabéu.'

'What?!' Vini said before he could stop himself. 'Okay, now we've really got to win this one!'

Vini was usually the team's most relaxed player, but even he felt the extra pressure in the build-up to facing Barcelona. He knew what it meant to the fans and the city.

In big games like this, it was always reassuring for Vini to have Marcelo playing behind him on the left wing. They had built a great understanding – and Marcelo was never shy about telling his friend when he needed to do a better job of tracking back.

The atmosphere at the Bernabéu on match day was always electric, but Vini got shivers when he walked out with his teammates for El Clásico. The crowd was a sea of white and the singing was louder than ever.

'Wow!' Vini said quietly to himself.

With the action swinging from end to end, Vini waited patiently for his chance. He stood strong as the tackles flew in and kept calling for the ball. He could feel the energy pick up in the crowd every time he ran at the Barcelona defence.

With twenty minutes to go, it was time for something special. Toni had the ball in midfield and spotted Vini in space on the left. At the same moment, they saw that the Barcelona full-back had switched off for a second. Toni pointed and Vini darted in behind.

Vini reached the ball first and suddenly he was in the box. He saw two Barcelona defenders hesitate – maybe they were expecting a cross, maybe they just didn't think Vini would shoot. Either way, Vini had a crucial yard of space.

He dribbled to get slightly closer to the Barcelona goal, then fired a quick shot towards the near post. He had wrong-footed the keeper at the last second and the ball flew into the net.

Goooooooooooooooooooooaaaaaaaaaaaaaaaaalllllllllllllll lllllllllllll!!!!!!!!!!!!!!!!!!

The Bernabéu erupted with the loudest cheer Vini had ever heard. He just ran towards the noise. It was all a blur – but it started to sink in as he looked up and saw all the fans standing and clapping. A goal in El Clásico!

On the scoreboard's big screen, Vini even spotted former Real star Cristiano Ronaldo clapping from the fancy VIP suites. Real struck again in stoppage time to seal a 2–0 win, but the night belonged to Vini. He couldn't stop grinning as he high-fived his teammates and soaked it all in. They were exhausted, but it felt so good to win El Clásico.

As Vini waited to speak to the reporters, a member of the Real media team appeared with a sheet of paper.

'You've made some history tonight,' he said. 'You've moved past Messi as the youngest scorer in El Clásico in the twenty-first century.'

He handed the sheet to Vini so he could see for himself. There it was: 19 years and 230 days.

'Nice!' Vini said, grinning. 'It was just amazing to see the stadium rocking like that. What a win!'

When he finally got back to the dressing room, he was showered with water as soon as he walked through the door.

'What a magic strike!' Marcelo said, putting an arm round Vini. 'That's the first of many Clásico goals, I'm sure!'

CHAPTER 18

THE CRISTIANO WORKOUTS

As Vini looked back on the previous six months, he could see the progress. His link-up play with his teammates was growing sharper every week and he was taking every chance to learn from the senior squad members.

But that all came to a sudden stop in 2020 when the COVID-19 global health crisis paused football seasons around the world. As Vini sat around the table with his friends and family, he was thankful that they were at least all together during this strange time.

It also meant that Vini had some extra time on his hands as he and his teammates waited for news on when the La Liga season might return.

Wesley and Luiz were usually available to play FIFA and there was always good food in the house, but Vini needed something else to keep him sharp. He was determined to get himself into even better shape for when the season restarted.

It was time to get serious about the Cristiano workouts. His former Real teammate was a fitness king – and it was one of the things that Vini had learned from being around Cristiano in the Real first team. He wanted every little advantage he could get.

Vini found all the details he needed for the workouts and set himself some weekly targets. He was excited to get started – even if his friends gave him a surprised look when he showed them his new plan.

'Does that say 6am?' Wesley asked, with a little grin. 'I think you've written that down wrong.'

Vini shook his head. 'Don't worry, you'll still be snoring, but I'll be up bright and early.'

When the alarm sounded, Vini sat up in bed and stretched his arms above his head. Time to get to work! Soon, he was running, jumping and lifting weights, then doing it all over again. Even when his muscles ached, he kept going. Before long, Wesley and Luiz were joining in and encouraging him.

'If it's good enough for Cristiano, it's good enough for me,' he told Luiz as he guzzled water and prepared for another set of sprints. 'When the season starts again, I'm going to be ready to dominate.'

He even hired a chef and made some changes to his diet, making sure that he had plenty of chicken, pasta and fish to stay healthy while he attacked his workouts.

Within a few weeks, Vini could feel the difference. He was even lighter on his feet and he now had more upper body strength to battle physical defenders. He could think of moments in games when he had been muscled off the ball – sometimes fairly, sometimes unfairly. That wouldn't be happening now!

Finally, after the restrictions from the global pandemic were lifted, La Liga was back, although games still had to take place without the fans, and Vini already knew that he would miss the buzz from the crowd. In the first training session with Real after the break, his teammates could instantly tell that Vini meant business.

In the first mini game, Vini dribbled forward and his touch got away from him. He sprinted to recover it, but Dani Carvajal got there at the same moment and they collided in a shoulder-to-shoulder bump. While Vini kept his balance, Dani bounced off him and landed on the ground. There were 'ooohs' from some of the coaches.

After passing the ball to Karim Benzema, Vini jogged back to help Dani up.

'Someone's been in the gym!' Dani said, patting Vini on the back. 'No one's going to be knocking you off the ball again this season.'

'I feel great,' Vini said. 'All the workouts have been fun, but nothing replaces the joy of being out there in a real game.'

Vini was realistic, though. Yes, he was fitter than he had ever been, but it would take more than that to earn a regular place in Zidane's team. Still, as he flicked a ball up onto his thigh and then set off dribbling around the coaches' cones, Vini was ready for the challenge.

CHAPTER 19

UPS AND DOWNS WITH ZIDANE

As Zidane read out the team for the upcoming Champions League game against Manchester City, Vini held his breath. Maybe, just maybe, he had done enough in training to prove he could make an impact in a bigger role. After all, Real were trailing in the tie and needed goals.

But he didn't hear his name.

He breathed out quietly, determined to be professional and keep a smile on his face, even though that was getting harder and harder to do. But Vini was still disappointed and upset. What more could he do to get a chance in the team? He had been asking himself that question for weeks.

As Zidane went through the tactics and some extra instructions, Vini took his phone out of his pocket and started reading through his messages.

That was a major no-no in team meetings, and Zidane was on it in a flash. He asked Vini to stay behind afterwards and made it very clear that his behaviour was unacceptable. 'After that, I can't let you play against City,' Zidane said. 'I'm sorry, but you know the rules.'

Vini apologised straightaway. He was so angry with himself. It was a silly mistake at the worst possible time, and now he wondered what this meant for his future in the first team.

Marcelo and Casemiro did their best to help him stay positive. 'Keep your head up,' Casemiro told him. 'It's a long season and things can change quickly.'

'You'll get another chance soon,' his father often reminded him. 'Support your teammates and work hard.'

Vini got even more serious about training. He was one of the first to arrive and one of the last to leave, focusing on his crossing and shooting. Nothing would get in his way. Yes, he had faced his share of criticism over the past year not just from Zidane, but also from Karim and the local newspapers in Madrid, but he had come too far to let that worry him. He just listened and tried to learn from it all.

It took some time to win Zidane's trust back, but Vini's positive attitude and clinical finishing in training were hard to ignore. Real reached the Champions League quarter-finals. Just before the start of a training session as part of preparations for the first leg, Zidane approached Vini.

'Vini, you're going to start tomorrow night,' Zidane said. 'We're going to take the game to Liverpool and you've earned this shot.'

As Zidane talked through more of the game plan with him, Vini got goosebumps. His manager was putting faith in him to deliver, and he was determined not to let him down.

That night, Vini felt just like he had before some of his first games for Flamengo and Real. The nerves were back and he couldn't sleep. If he had a bad game against Liverpool, when might he get another chance?

He tried to block that thought out of his mind. He reminded himself that if he played well, it could be the big breakthrough moment in his Real career.

It was still an odd feeling, due to the global pandemic, not to see fans in the stands as he walked out onto the pitch at an empty Bernabéu, but in any case, Vini would need no extra boost from a crowd that night. He jogged over to the touchline with one of the warm-up balls. Zidane was waiting for him, and gave him a high-five. 'Make those runs,' he said. 'There's space behind this Liverpool defence and none of their defenders can catch you.'

Vini nodded and kept reminding himself about those instructions. He quickly saw that his manager was right – he would be most dangerous making runs for a pass over the top. The Liverpool defence was often pushing up to the halfway line, hoping to catch Real offside.

When Toni got the ball deep in Real's half, Vini held his run and then set off. He knew what was coming. But somehow the Liverpool defence didn't. Toni's long pass floated forward and Vini was onto it in a flash.

He watched the ball carefully, took it down on his chest and kept running. He was in the box now and there was no chance of a Liverpool player recovering to make a block. He took a second to check the angle and then drilled a low shot into the net. 1–0!

Gooooooooooooooooooooaaaaaaaaaaaaaaaaalllllllllllllll llllllllllll!!!!!!!!!!!!!!!!!!!!

Vini glanced over at the assistant referee. There was no flag. He had timed the run perfectly. In some ways, it was the simplest of goals – one long ball, one touch to control it, and bang. Vini pointed to the Real badge and imagined what it would have been like with thousands of fans screaming when the shot went in.

Marco made it 2–0, but there was still a long way to go and Liverpool were dangerous. 'Don't relax!' Zidane reminded them at half-time. 'Keep the ball and look for Vini whenever he's one-on-one against their defenders.'

Liverpool quickly pulled a goal back, but there was no panic. Vini fed off the calmness of Luka and Toni. They just got on with the game, and he did the same. Real attacked down the right and Vini was the only white shirt in the box. He wasn't going to win a header against the Liverpool centre-backs so he stayed in a deeper position and waited for the right moment.

Luka drifted away from his marker and sped into the box. More Liverpool defenders rushed to close him down, and Vini saw his chance. He darted into space to create room for a pass. 'Square it, Luka,' he called.

As always, Luka's pass was just right and Vini didn't need to take a touch to control it. He just swung his right foot and watched the ball go past the Liverpool keeper's dive and into the bottom corner. 3–1!

Goooooooooooooooooooaaaaaaaaaaaaaaaallllllllllllll llllllllllll!!!!!!!!!!!!!!!!!!

Vini spun away, jumping with excitement. What a night! He really needed this moment – and it felt like an even bigger breakthrough when Zidane reached over to congratulate him during the celebrations.

Those huge goals gave Vini an energy boost for the rest of the season. Everything was moving in the right direction, but he would take nothing for granted.

CHAPTER 20

TASTING THE COPA AMÉRICA

Vini could still remember the first Copa América tournament that he had seen as a kid. Those were great memories, watching the games with his dad and Uncle Ulysses and seeing their reactions whenever Brazil scored. The World Cup would always be the number one prize, but the Copa América winners were the champions of South America. That counted for a lot too.

As the defending Copa América champions, Brazil had high expectations. When didn't they? Vini knew there would always be pressure to deliver for a country with such a long football history. Most of all, though, he was thrilled to be in the squad for the

2021 tournament.

Earning regular minutes would be tough, though. He knew there was major competition for places in the starting line-up. Tite had often picked Neymar and Richarlison up front, so Vini understood that he might have to settle for a super sub role.

In the group game against Ecuador, Vini could see from the bench that Tite was getting frustrated with the team's performance. They were struggling to break down a physical Ecuador defence. Eventually, he turned around to face the bench and pointed at Vini.

'Get ready,' he said.

Vini didn't need to be told twice. He scurried down to the touchline and went through another round of stretches and jumps.

Neymar gave him a pat on the back as he ran over to the left wing. 'Stay out wide and I'll get the ball to you,' he called.

Vini couldn't help Brazil find a winning goal, but the experience was incredible. He looked around the dressing room after the game and let it all sink in. So that was the Copa América!

Brazil powered on, winning 1–0 over both Chile and Peru. In the final, they faced Argentina with the Copa América trophy up for grabs. On TV, it was all about Neymar vs. Messi, but Vini knew it would be about much more than that.

There were huge expectations by now. Brazil had looked so good on their way to the final, but those on the bench fell silent when Argentina took the lead. Suddenly, the Brazilians were in trouble. With thirty minutes to go, Vini was one of the subs that Tite sent on to try to rescue the game.

Vini's teammates got the ball out to him at every opportunity, and he showed no fear of running at the Argentina defence. He lost the ball the first few times, but he didn't get discouraged. His next run created a great chance for Gabi, another of the Brazil substitutes. He watched as Gabi controlled his clever through ball, but the Argentina keeper made a good save. So close!

Argentina had seen enough to be worried now. As Vini danced forward again, their right-back hacked him down. 'We're rattling them!' Vini shouted, grinning.

But this wasn't to be Brazil's year. Despite all
the late pressure, they just ran out of time. As the
Argentina players rushed to celebrate with Lionel
Messi, Vini sat on the pitch, stunned. It was a tearful
Brazil dressing room and a very quiet ride back to the
hotel. As Vini sat on the team bus and looked out of
the window, he promised himself that he would make
amends for this loss. He would get back to another
Copa América final and win the trophy.

It was too soon to think too much about the future,
but the past month had given Vini another taste of
what it meant to wear the famous yellow Brazil shirt –
the joy of wins and the pain of losses. As he returned
to Madrid, he could feel that missing out on Copa
América glory had made him even hungrier to win big
trophies.

CHAPTER 21

THE ANCELOTTI EFFECT

Despite some memorable highlights, Vini still had some questions about his future as he returned to Real for the 2021–22 season. Over the summer, there had been more changes. Zidane had left the club, and Carlo Ancelotti was the new manager. For Vini, Ancelotti's arrival brought different possibilities and a whole new feeling in training.

'It's good to be back!' Carlo started, with a big smile. He had enjoyed great success as Real boss several years before and was already settling back in. 'We've got a lot of work ahead of us, but I'm really excited about this adventure.'

In the first few training sessions, Carlo watched in

amazement as Vini turned defenders inside out and seemed to have an endless supply of turns, tricks and flicks. Carlo knew the history too.

'Amazing work out there,' he told Vini during a quick break. 'Listen, I know it's been a bit of a roller-coaster for you at Real so far, and I've seen how tough it can be for youngsters to join a big club like this. But I can't wait to work with you. You've got so much talent and my job is to give you the confidence and support to shine.'

Those words meant everything to Vini. He felt the pressure and disappointments wash away, replaced with a hunger to get better every day. With Carlo's guidance, he truly believed he could become one of the best players in the world.

He was in the perfect team too. Real's midfielders could keep the ball for days with their effortless passing, and Vini's speed and movement gave the team something different. He had played with Luka, Toni and Karim for long enough now to know exactly where he needed to be. If he made the runs, they would find him.

As the 2021–22 season kicked off, Vini made
a flying start – just as he knew he would. He had
worked so hard on his end product after Zidane's
advice, and now it was all coming together at the right
time.

Vini scored against Alavés in the first game of the
season, slotting home a simple finish from Karim's
cross. But a bigger test awaited the next week as
Vini came off the bench, with Real losing 2–1 against
Levante.

'Just do what you do,' Carlo told him on the
touchline. 'But don't drop too deep. Stay right on the
shoulder of the last defender.'

Vini got a few easy touches to catch up with the
speed of the game, then he started making runs to
stretch the Levante defence.

'That's it!' Carlo called, pointing at Vini and
clapping after he made a quick diagonal run from the
left into the middle. The long pass towards him had
been overhit, but it was the right idea.

Then Casemiro controlled a loose ball in midfield
and looked up. Vini knew that was his cue to start

sprinting again. Sure enough, Casemiro spotted
him and swept the ball forward behind the Levante
defence.

Vini was in the clear. He could sense two defenders
chasing him, but he stayed calm and placed a low left-
footed shot under the keeper. 2–2!

*Goooooooooooooooooooaaaaaaaaaaaaaaaalllllllllllllll
llllllllllll!!!!!!!!!!!!!!!!!!!*

He jumped and punched the air in celebration. But
the good feelings didn't last long as Levante quickly
made it 3–2. Now Real had to do it all again.

The white shirts flew forward. With five minutes to
go, Vini made another run, just to the left of Karim.
'Slide it through!' he screamed.

He took the pass with his right foot and angled
his body just enough to whip a shot towards the far
corner. He watched as if it was slow motion. The ball
curled back, bounced off the post and into the net.
3–3!

*Goooooooooooooooooooaaaaaaaaaaaaaaaalllllllllllllll
llllllllllll!!!!!!!!!!!!!!!!!!!*

'You've saved us!' Karim shouted, high-fiving Vini

as he scooped up the ball and rushed back to the halfway line.

Carlo loved what he saw. Vini had changed the game in the second half with his pace and movement. Carlo knew what that meant. From now on, he had to think of Vini as a starter, not a sub.

The goals and assists kept coming for Vini as Real got on a winning run. 'We're the team to beat,' he told Karim. 'We could really win La Liga and the Champions League this season!'

But there were still some tough moments mixed in with all Vini's highlights. In some away games, fans screamed insults at him. He brushed most of that off. He had faced that ever since getting into the Flamengo first team and being singled out as a future star.

But some of the insults were different. Some of them were about the colour of his skin and those hurt him deeply. There was no place for that behaviour in football – or anywhere in life. Vini knew he had to speak up and he reported what he had experienced.

Through all of those challenges, it was a relief to feel so settled in the Real team. His teammates had become like an extra part of his family, and with Carlo helping his decision-making and calmness on the pitch, Vini felt unstoppable.

CHAPTER 22

THE COMEBACK KINGS

'Facing Messi, Neymar and Mbappé is what the Champions League is all about,' Vini said to Wesley and Luiz as they played a Real Madrid vs. PSG game on the FIFA video game.

A few weeks later, the teams were playing in real life too.

'Let's make this our year!' Carlo said as the Real squad gathered for that Champions League Round of 16 matchup against PSG. 'Never stop believing. With the talent in this room, you can achieve anything.'

But the Champions League dream was hanging by a thread when PSG won the first leg in France and Kylian Mbappé gave them a 1–0 lead at the Bernabéu.

Vini remembered Carlo's words, though. Until the final whistle, this team always had a chance.

In the second half, Vini made a flying start, making runs and stretching the defence. When he saw Karim pressuring the PSG keeper, he ran forward in case there was a bad clearance. He was rewarded when the ball skimmed his way. Rather than rushing a shot at the open goal, he took a touch and laid it across to Karim for a tap-in. Game on!

Suddenly, there was panic in the PSG defence. Karim reacted first to a great pass from Luka. Real were level again.

'Keep pressing them!' Carlo shouted. 'We've got them on the ropes.'

From the kick-off, Vini sprinted forward to deny PSG any easy passes. His pressure forced another mistake. A bad pass went straight to Karim, and he steered a quick shot into the bottom corner.

'Whoa!' Vini screamed, jumping and punching the air in celebration. 'What a comeback!'

On his way back for the kick-off, he saw the looks on the faces of Messi, Neymar and Mbappé. They were stunned. Real hung on in the final minutes to book their place in the quarter-finals.

'When we play like that, we're unstoppable!' Vini called to Luka and Karim.

'There's something really special about this team,' Carlo said once the dressing room party had calmed down a little. 'I'm so proud to coach you. You've got the football ability but you're warriors too. You never give up.'

Despite all the celebrations, Vini had to remind himself that there was still a long road ahead if Real wanted to lift the trophy. That battle with PSG had felt like three rounds in one, but they couldn't afford to overlook Chelsea in the quarter-finals.

The first leg was all about Karim, who stole the show with a hat-trick. But Vini played his part. He got the ball with a Chelsea defender backing off and sprung into life. With a quick touch, he laid it inside to Karim and sprinted forward for the one-two. Karim set him free with a flicked pass and he flew towards the Chelsea goal. The angle was too tight for a shot, but Vini took a look to see where his strike partner was and then floated in the perfect cross. Karim powered a header into the top corner.

'Let's go!!!' Vini screamed as Karim raced towards him, celebrating with the Real fans.

With four touches, Vini and Karim had cut through the Chelsea defence. Three minutes later, Karim doubled the lead with another brilliant header from Luka's cross.

Karim finished off his hat-trick after a howler from the Chelsea keeper, and Vini sprinted over to celebrate. With a 3–1 lead from the away leg, Real were within touching distance of the semi-finals. But Carlo reminded his team that he had seen some big leads slip away in this tournament. The Real players themselves had dug their way out of some deep holes.

Despite Carlo's warnings, Real struggled at home in the second leg. Chelsea were already 2–0 up – and with fifteen minutes to go, they scored again. Real were heading out. 'Come on!' Vini shouted. 'We've got to wake up!' Luckily, Luka had a moment of magic up his sleeve. With one flick of the outside of his right boot, he curled in the perfect cross for

Rodrygo to score.

As the game was becoming even more open in extra time, Vini knew he had one more big run left. Real won the ball back in midfield and a clipped pass released Vini on the left. He raced forward but he didn't rush the cross. He knew this might be one of their last good scoring chances.

There were five Chelsea shirts in the box and just two white Real shirts, but Vini knew where Karim would be. He dinked the cross towards the penalty spot, and Karim dived forward to head the ball into the bottom corner.

Real held on with some desperate defending to survive another near exit. After the final whistle, Vini and Federico jogged around the pitch as the fans cheered. But there was part joy, part relief. 'We almost blew that!' Vini said.

'You guys just love making things hard for yourselves,' Carlo said, shaking his head and grinning.

The semi-finals would be even tougher. It was Real Madrid vs. Manchester City, and fans all over the world were counting the days.

'We can't afford to relax for even a few minutes against Manchester City,' Carlo said. 'They're too good for that.'

Though Real were playing away from the Bernabéu for the first leg, it felt good to know that they would have home support in the second leg. But after eleven minutes, it looked like Real might already be on their way out. Vini looked up at the sky in shock as City powered 2–0 ahead.

'Let's get back to playing Real Madrid football!' he called, urging the defence to settle down. City looked like scoring every time they attacked.

Karim pulled a goal back with a first-time finish, but City scored again just after half-time, intercepting a pass that was meant for Vini and punishing Real. Vini had his hands on his head. Should he have been stronger when the ball was played up to him?

Real needed another spark – and Vini provided it. He was up against Fernandinho on the left wing and Vini knew him well from the Brazil squad. Fernandinho had been marking him tightly all game, so Vini decided to use that to his advantage. On the next pass up the line, instead of controlling the ball, Vini just let the ball roll through his legs and spun away behind Fernandinho, who had been expecting Vini to take a touch.

There was lots of space in behind and no defenders in sight. Vini raced forward, cutting in a little from the left with the angle of his run. The City defenders were so worried about Vini crossing the ball to Karim that they kept backing off. Vini just ran forward until he had the angle he wanted and placed a low shot perfectly in the bottom corner.

Goooooooooooooooooooaaaaaaaaaaaaaaaallllllllllllll llllllllllll!!!!!!!!!!!!!!!!!!!!

'I wanted to cross it to you at first,' Vini said as Karim hugged him. 'But they just let me run right into the box!'

Real were back in it. But they never looked solid at the back – and City scored a fourth, and then almost got a fifth. In the final ten minutes, they got a lifeline from a City handball in the box. Karim stepped up to score the penalty.

After a roller-coaster night, Real had somehow

clawed their way back to 4–3 and that looked like a decent result to take back to the Bernabéu. Carlo clapped his players off. Vini was exhausted but dragged himself over to see the travelling Real fans. They were one big performance away from the final.

But City had the upper hand in Madrid, frustrating Vini and Karim. When City took the lead in the second half, Vini knew Real had a mountain to climb. But again they kept battling. Rodrygo equalised from Karim's cross, and Vini had his hands in the air. There was still a chance! He ran to get the ball out of the net for the kick-off, but the clock was already at ninety minutes.

It was now or never. Real swung another cross into the box and the City defenders were out of position. Rodrygo was in the right place at the right time again. He leapt to head the ball into the net. 2–1! Vini sprinted over. 'We're the comeback kings!' he screamed, hugging Rodrygo and telling the crowd to get even louder. This was the most unbelievable fightback he had ever been part of.

Now City were rocking. Early in extra-time, Karim

was fouled in the box. 'Penalty!' Vini yelled. The
referee agreed, and Karim made no mistake. From the
brink of elimination, Real were ahead.

The next twenty-five minutes felt like two hours. At
last, he heard the final whistle. The Bernabéu erupted
into cheers and chants. Vini and Real were into the
Champions League final!

'I'm running out of things to say!' Carlo joked. 'I
don't think I've ever seen a fightback like that one
tonight. You're lions, all of you! What a performance!'

Vini was in dreamland these days. Real had
clinched the La Liga title a week earlier and he had
played a huge part in that success with seventeen
goals and thirteen assists. Now he had a Champions
League final to win.

Liverpool stood in their way, but Vini was confident
after scoring twice against them the year before. 'I
think we've been counted out of the Champions
League about five different times this season,' Carlo
said, smiling and making everyone in the dressing
room relax a little. 'We've done it the hard way but
let's finish the job in style.'

After a tense first half, Vini could tell Real were going to have to dig deep again if they wanted to lift the trophy. Liverpool created chances and Vini held his breath as Thibaut made save after save.

Then Federico burst forward on the right. Vini darted inside from the left wing, trying to time his run. He saw Federico decide to shoot, or maybe to cross. Vini wasn't sure, but he had a good sense of where the ball was going.

When Federico fired the ball across the box, Vini reacted quickest, while the Liverpool defenders just stood and watched. He followed the path of the ball. It was going wide, but he arrived just in time to steer a shot into the net.

Goooooooooooooooooooooaaaaaaaaaaaaaaaaalllllllllllllll lllllllllllll!!!!!!!!!!!!!!!!!!!!

Vini's first thought was that he might be offside. Liverpool were appealing, but the VAR replay showed that Vini was just onside. The celebrations could begin and all the Real subs raced over to jump on his back. He kissed the Real badge on his shirt as the fans leapt up and down.

In the end, it was the winning goal! Real had to ride their luck, Thibaut made more saves and then it was over. Vini just wanted to hug everyone. 'We've done it!' he screamed as he spotted Carlo and ran over.

For Vini, seeing the Champions League winner's medal round his neck was an incredible feeling. He couldn't stop staring at it. Then Marcelo was handed the trophy and he walked over to where Vini and his teammates were already singing and dancing. Marcelo lifted it high in the air and fireworks flew into the sky behind the Real players.

As the trophy was passed from player to player, Vini waited patiently. Finally, he got it. It was such a beautiful trophy and he could hardly believe that he was holding it. Even more, he could hardly believe that he had scored the winning goal. The celebrations went on late into the night and Vini knew this run to Champions League glory was right up there with the proudest moments of his life.

CHAPTER 23

WORLD CUP HEARTBREAK

'This is our big chance,' Vini said to Casemiro as they boarded the plane for the 2022 World Cup in Qatar. It was a strange feeling to be going to a World Cup tournament in November instead of the summer, but Vini hoped the timing would work in Brazil's favour.

Most people viewed them as the favourites to lift the trophy, with Vini up front alongside Neymar and Richarlison, Casemiro in midfield and Thiago Silva at the back. Brazil had a lot of great attackers, but Vini felt good about his chances of staying in the starting line-up – and scoring his first international goal against Chile at the Maracanā Stadium earlier in the year had given him even more confidence.

From the minute the plane landed in Qatar, Vini saw lots of fans in yellow Brazil shirts – they were all desperate for a glimpse of the players and counting on this squad to end the national team's disappointing twenty-year stretch at the World Cup. Vini had watched the tournaments in 2010, 2014 and 2018, as one of those fans who stopped everything to watch the Brazil games, but he was now part of the excitement sweeping the country.

It was a confident, experienced Brazil squad, but there were always surprises at big tournaments. 'We need to be focused and organised,' Tite explained on the first day of training in Qatar. 'We're always going to play with style, but we've got to back it up with toughness.'

As the players warmed up before the opening match against Serbia, Vini dribbled the ball over to where Neymar and Richarlison were standing. 'What a feeling!' he said, looking from one end of the stadium to the other. 'I can picture all the Brazil fans back at home crowded round the TV.'

'It's going to get pretty loud in here too!' Neymar

replied. 'Did you see all the yellow shirts in the streets around the stadium?'

Vini nodded and grinned. 'Well, we better put on a show for them then!'

The walk down the tunnel and out onto the pitch was one of the proudest moments of Vini's life. He took a deep breath and tried to stay calm with all the emotions bubbling up inside him. This was the dream – playing for Brazil at the World Cup. This is what he had worked so hard for.

The first half finished 0–0, but Vini could feel Brazil slowly taking over the game. 'We're starting to find little holes in their defence,' Tite reassured his players, sensing some of the disappointment in the dressing room. 'Stay patient and get the ball out wide.'

Vini grinned to himself. Getting the ball out wide meant more opportunities for him to run at defenders and dip into his box of tricks.

He worked hard to keep the Serbia defenders guessing – sometimes dropping deep for a pass, sometimes sprinting in behind for a ball over the top. As Neymar set off on a mazy run, Vini drifted into the box. Neymar skipped past another tackle, but the ball ran free. Vini had an instant to decide whether to get out of the way so that Neymar could stretch for a shot on his left foot or step towards the ball and take a shot himself.

He chose the second option, shouting 'Vini's ball' and then smashing a low shot. The Serbia keeper could only push the ball out in front of him, and Richarlison was there to score the rebound.

Yes!!! Vini ran first to Neymar then to Richarlison. This was a team goal and they had all played their part.

Now Serbia had to push more players forward. Space quickly opened up and Vini raced clear on the left wing, with two defenders struggling to keep up. He took his time and clipped a cross towards Richarlison.

'Go on, big man!' he thought to himself as he watched Richarlison control the cross and start to swivel for an acrobatic shot. The next second, the net bulged. 2–0. Vini put both arms in the air. It was a classic Brazilian move.

Brazil had to work hard to beat Switzerland 1–0, then rested Vini and other key players for the final group game against Cameroon. Although they cruised through to the second round, the mood in the Brazil camp wasn't all positive. Neymar's ankle injury was a big concern, and Vini crossed his fingers that his teammate would be back for the knockout rounds.

'Either way, I'll just have to do more,' Vini told himself.

Now all his attention was on South Korea, Brazil's opponents in the first knockout round. Vini listened carefully as Tite walked through the game plan and the other coaches showed video clips of South Korea's group games. Suddenly, there was more pressure. Unlike the group games, there was no safety net now. One bad performance and Brazil would be packing their bags.

'Don't look too far ahead,' Tite had told the players at the start of the tournament. That was especially true now.

Vini felt great from the moment he woke up on game day. That carried on through the warm-up. He had proven himself with good performances in the group stage, and now he wanted to show he could deliver in World Cup knockout games too.

'Get the ball moving early,' Tite said, as the players sat at their lockers with their yellow shirts already on. 'Take control before they have a chance to settle.'

Neymar high-fived Vini as they headed for the tunnel. 'Welcome back, buddy,' Vini said, relieved that his teammate was fit enough to return.

As the thousands of Brazil fans in the stands roared the team on, Vini delivered the perfect start. Raphinha broke free on the right wing and, for once, Vini didn't break into a full sprint. He saw that Neymar and Richarlison were already bursting towards the near post, so he waited at the back post.

Raphinha fizzed the ball across and, after Neymar couldn't reach it, it landed perfectly at Vini's feet. He didn't take his eyes off the goal, though he could sense two or three South Korea defenders rushing to block his shot. Vini cushioned the ball with one touch and dinked a clever finish through the crowd of bodies and into the net.

*Goooooooooooooooooooaaaaaaaaaaaaaaaallllllllllllll
llllllllllll!!!!!!!!!!!!!!!!!!!!*

The whole Brazil team joined in the celebrations,
burying Vini in hugs. In front of a large section of
Brazilian fans, Vini stood with Raphinha and Neymar
and then broke into a dance routine that sent the
cheering up another level.

Neymar doubled the lead with a penalty, then
Richarlison made it 3–0. Now even Tite was taking
part in the dancing. To complete a dazzling first half,
Vini found space on the left and served up an inch-
perfect cross for Lucas Paquetá to thump home a
fourth goal.

At half-time, Tite was almost speechless. 'What
else can I say?' he told the team, with his arms
outstretched. 'That was one of the most magical forty-
five minutes I've ever seen.'

When Brazil played like that, no one could stop
them. The game finished 4–1, but Vini had done the
damage in the first half. Now Croatia awaited them in
the quarter-finals. That meant a showdown with Luka,
with Real Madrid bragging rights on the line.

Unlike South Korea, Croatia didn't leave big gaps for Brazil to fly forward. Instead, Vini spent a lot of the first half dropping deep to try to win the ball back as Luka glided around midfield. Even when he did get the ball, there always seemed to be two or three red-and-white Croatia shirts around him.

His heart sank in the second half when the referee stopped the game for a substitution. Rodrygo was coming on and Vini saw his Number 10 on the electronic board. He jogged off, high-fived Rodrygo and found a seat on the bench. He just wished he was still on the pitch helping his teammates.

The game finished goalless after ninety minutes and headed into extra-time. Vini was just a spectator now and he could feel his heart thumping every time Brazil pushed forward.

Then Neymar produced a moment of magic. 'Go on!' Vini said to himself as Neymar set off running. 'Go on!' he called louder as Neymar got a return pass, swayed away from two defenders, went round the keeper and slotted the ball into the net.

'Yes!!!!' Vini screamed, jumping up and hugging the

subs next to him.

He looked up at the scoreboard. There were only fifteen minutes to go. 'Semi-finals, here we come!' he thought to himself.

But it was as if the Brazil players on the pitch had the same thought. They lost focus and Croatia stunned the partying crowd with a deflected equaliser. Vini sat completely still, mouth open. What had just happened?

Now a penalty shootout would decide the game – and Vini wouldn't get to take one. All he could do was wish the penalty takers good luck and huddle together with the substitutes and coaches.

Neymar scored. Luka scored. Rodrygo's penalty was saved by the Croatia keeper, who was having the night of his life. More penalties flew into the net. Now Marquinhos had to score. He hit the post.

The Croatia players raced across the pitch to celebrate. Vini put his head in his hands. It wasn't supposed to end like this. With his head still spinning, he went to see his teammates – they were all crushed.

Eventually, they all dragged themselves back to

a silent dressing room. Tite said a few words about being proud of them and how cruel penalties could be. But he mostly left them to their thoughts. Vini and the Brazil squad had arrived in Qatar on a mission to lift the trophy – they had fallen short this time. They could only look on as rivals Argentina went on to reach the final, which they won on penalties.

'I know it stings now, but you'll be even stronger after this,' Tite said, walking with Vini to the team bus. 'Let this drive you on. Brazil is counting on you to help lead the next generation.'

Vini nodded. Even he couldn't manage a smile that night, but he appreciated his coach's words. One thing was for certain: he was now more determined than ever to bring the World Cup trophy home to Brazil.

With the unusual winter World Cup timing, Vini planned to take a few days to clear his head and then it would be time to get back to Madrid to continue the Real trophy chase. He found a seat near the back of the bus, put on his headphones and closed his eyes. Vini had proved a lot of things to a lot of people over the past few years. Now he was one of the main men, both at Real Madrid and for Brazil. It still seemed like only yesterday that he was fighting for his future at Real and waiting for a chance to impress for Brazil. 'Things really do move at lightning speed in the football world,' he told his parents as they sat together for lunch.

'What's incredible is that you haven't even reached your peak yet,' his dad replied. 'You're still only twenty-two. Imagine the player you'll be in five years' time!'

Vini grinned. He was doing a lot of that lately. 'Hopefully I'll have won so many trophies that I need an extra room to display them all!'

It barely seemed real at times. His journey from the challenges of São Gonçalo to major trophies and a big contract at Real Madrid plus a regular place in the Brazil team. 'It's a fairytale story,' Vini told his friends as they talked about the old days in Brazil. 'I don't know how else to describe it.'

All the success was great, but Vini was always looking for the next challenge – and there were plenty more to come. After signing a new contract with Real that would run through to 2027, he knew that this was where he wanted to be.

He was the future for his club and for his country. At Real, Karim and Luka were nearing the end of their amazing careers. For Brazil, Neymar was uncertain about his international future and other older players would be retiring. The stage was set for Vini to dominate.

'It's all ahead of you, my friend,' Marcelo told him when they met up after the World Cup. 'You've got to take the torch now, for Real and Brazil. If you keep working hard, you've got the chance to become one of the all-time greats.'

'I like the sound of that,' Vini said, smiling like only he could. 'Bring it on.'

Read on for a sneak preview of
another brilliant football story by
Matt and Tom Oldfield. . .

MODRIC

Available now!

CHAPTER 1

CHAMPIONS LEAGUE
WINNER

24 May 2014, Estádio da Luz, Lisbon

After nine months of amazing football action, it was time for Europe's biggest match – the Champions League Final!

An incredible 60,000 fans clapped and cheered as the two teams walked out of the tunnel, past the shiny silver trophy, and onto the pitch.

Atléti! Atléti! Atléti!

On one side were Atlético Madrid, wearing their red-and-white stripes. The new Champions of Spain were a very tough team to beat.

Real! Real! Real!

On the other side were their Madrid rivals, the
Galácticos, wearing their blue tracksuit tops. The TV
cameras moved along their line of superstars:

Ángel Di María, Gareth Bale, Sami Khedira, Raphaël
Varane, Karim Benzema, Cristiano Ronaldo…

Tucked in between these footballing giants was
Luka, Real Madrid's little midfield maestro. Luka
might not have looked that big, but he was as brave as
a lion. Alongside Sami, it would be his job to win the
ball and pass it forward to Real's fantastic forwards.

'This is our year, lads!' Real's captain Iker Casillas
called out before kick-off. 'Let's win *La Décima!*'

The Real Madrid fans had been waiting twelve long
years to win their tenth Champions League title. They
were getting desperate! But after losing in the semi-
finals for three years in a row, their team had, at last,
made it all the way to the final once again. Now, they
just had to win it.

From the very first minute, Luka controlled the
game calmly for Real. It was his first-ever Champions
League final but it didn't look that way. What a

natural!

Control, turn, perfect pass,

Control, turn, perfect pass,

Control, turn, dribble, then perfect pass!

Luka was always looking to create a goalscoring chance but he never rushed his pass. Patience was key. Eventually, a gap would appear in the Atlético defence.

At five-feet, eight-inches, Luka was one of the smallest players on the pitch, but what did size matter with so much spirit? He made tackles, intercepted passes, and he even won headers!

In the thirty-sixth minute, however, Atlético took the lead. Luka could only watch as Diego Godín's header looped up over Iker's outstretched arm. *1–0!*

'Keep going!' the Real centre-back Sergio Ramos urged his teammates. 'We've got plenty of time to grab an equaliser.'

Luka wasn't the kind of player to panic. He just kept doing what he always did, pushing Real Madrid up the pitch.

Control, turn, perfect pass,

Control, turn, perfect pass,
Control, turn, dribble, then perfect pass!

But as the second half flew by, Real still hadn't scored. Thibaut Courtois saved Cristiano's free kick. Karim shot wide, then Isco, then Gareth.

'How many chances do we need?' Luka groaned, reading the minds of all the anxious Real Madrid supporters in the stands.

When he raced over to take a corner, the match was deep into injury time. It was now or never in the Champions League final…

Luka curled a beautiful cross towards the penalty spot and hoped for the best. There was lots of pushing and shoving in the box but suddenly, Sergio sprang up and headed the ball into the net. *1–1!*

Over by the corner flag, Luka threw his arms up triumphantly. 'We did it!' he roared.

What a goal, and what a time to score it! The Atlético players were distraught; the Real players were delighted. Their *Décima* dream was still alive.

In extra time, Real raced away to victory. Ángel's shot was saved, but Gareth was in the right place to score the rebound. *2–1!*

'Yes!' Luka screamed as he celebrated with his old Tottenham teammate.

This was why they had both moved to Real Madrid – for the glory, for the trophies. When it came to winning, the team was totally ruthless.

Marcelo dribbled forward and shot past Courtois. *3–1!*

Cristiano scored from the penalty spot. *4–1!*

Luka bounced up and down with his brilliant teammates in front of the Real Madrid fans. They were the new Champions of Europe!

After a bad start, it had turned out to be the best night of Luka's life by far. He had a Croatian flag wrapped around his shoulders, a winners' medal around his neck, and soon, he would have the Champions League trophy in his hands!

But first, it was Iker's turn. As the Real Madrid captain lifted the cup high above his head, clouds of white confetti filled the sky. It was time to get the party started.

Campeones, Campeones, Olé! Olé! Olé!

When the trophy finally reached Luka, he held on tightly. Wow, it was huge, and quite heavy too. Imagine if he dropped it!

'Hurray!' he yelled up into the Lisbon night sky.

It was a moment that Luka would treasure forever. He was a football superstar now. He knew that his grandad would be so proud of him.

CHAPTER 2

GOAT HERDING WITH GRANDAD

'Luka!' a tired voice shouted through the open back door. 'Where are you? I need your help please. We've got work to do.'

'Coming, Grandad!' Luka replied, remembering to grab his coat off the hook before he rushed outside. In winter, it could be bitterly cold on the slopes of the Velebit mountain range where the Modrić family lived.

'Good boy,' his grandad said, giving him a hearty pat on the back. 'Right, let's go.'

As Luka walked beside his grandad, he didn't look up at the wild, lonely landscape that surrounded them. He was used to those views. It was his home, after all. Instead, he kept his head down, looking at the path ahead. He did this for two reasons. The first reason was that the ground was rocky and uneven, and he didn't want to trip and fall. The second reason was that he was searching for the perfect stick.

Luka couldn't herd goats without a good stick – no way! That would be like asking a footballer to play without a football.

'Not bad,' his grandad said, nodding approvingly when Luka showed him the stick he had chosen. 'That will do nicely.'

Luka was still only five years old but that was old enough to go goat herding with his grandad. Besides, if he didn't help out, who else could? There weren't any kind neighbours nearby; their house was the only house on the street. And Luka's parents, Stipe and Radojka, were too busy working long hours in a local knitwear factory in order to earn money for the family.

So, goat herding was Luka's job and he took it very seriously. That's why picking the perfect stick was so important.

'No, wrong way!' Luka told any goats that tried to take a different route. He was still very small but he was brave enough to block their path. 'That's it – follow your brothers and sisters!'

It was so peaceful up on the mountain paths. Most of the time, it was just Luka, the goats, and Grandad. What in the world could be better than that? There weren't many other young children in the area, so Grandad was his best friend. As they walked, the old man told lots of exciting stories about his life, and Luka listened carefully, taking in every word.

'But now, the times are changing,' his grandad often warned on their goat-herding adventures together. 'Trouble is on its way.'

Unfortunately, Luka's grandad turned out to be right about that. First came war and sorrow, and then came football and joy.

CHAPTER 3

THE SORROWS OF WAR

On a cold December day in 1991, just a week before Christmas, Luka's grandad led the goats along the mountain slopes as usual. This time, however, he was alone because Luka was busy learning at school. And, sadly, their homeland was no longer a peaceful place.

Their country, Croatia, was fighting fiercely to become an independent nation, separate from Yugoslavia. Yugoslavia, however, weren't going to let them leave without a fight. On that cold December day, soldiers suddenly stormed the village of Modrići, and Luka's grandad was killed.

When he returned from school and heard the tragic

news, Luka was absolutely devastated. He loved
his grandad so much and now they would never be
able to goat herd together again. How could such a
horrible thing happen to his poor, innocent grandad?
War was a very difficult thing for a six-year-old child to
understand.

'I'm so sorry, Luka,' his mum told him tearfully, 'but
we have to leave this place straight away. It's not safe
to stay here any longer.'

Their happy days in Modrići were over; now, they
were refugees on the run. The family quickly packed up
their belongings and moved to Zadar, the nearest city,
where Luka and his sister Jasmina had been born.

What now? They had nowhere to live, and they
didn't have enough money to rent a new house of
their own. Fortunately, they were offered a small,
bare room in the Hotel Kolovare. They didn't have
electricity or running water, but at least they had a
shelter from the war.

But even in Zadar, things were far from safe. All
through the day and through the night, Luka and
his family lived with the loud sounds of war. Even

walking out into the streets was a dangerous thing to do. As the fight for independence went on, there was more and more damage everywhere. They were tough and terrible times for the Croatian nation.

'One day, everything will be peaceful again,' Luka's mum promised them as they huddled together to keep warm.

But when? Luka wanted to go back to Modrići. In Zadar, he was only an hour's drive from his old home, but it felt like a lifetime away. It was such a shock to go from the quiet of the countryside to the noise and bustle of a city. Compared to Modrići, Zadar felt really big and scary. There were strange, sad faces everywhere he looked.

'Dad, when are we going back home?' Luka asked again and again.

'We can't, son,' Stipe always replied, his face full of sorrow. 'This is our home now.'

Luka never stopped missing Modrići, the mountains, the goats and most of all, his grandad. But luckily, he found a new love that helped him to escape from the sorrows of war...

VINÍCIUS JNR

20 THE FACTS

NAME: Vinícius José Paixão de Oliveira Júnior

DATE OF BIRTH: 12 July 2000

PLACE OF BIRTH: São Gonçalo

NATIONALITY: Brazilian

BEST FRIENDS: Rodrygo and Karim Benzema

CURRENT CLUB: Real Madrid

POSITION: Left Winger

THE STATS

Height (cm):	176
Club appearances:	294
Club goals:	79
Club assists:	73
Club trophies:	9
International appearances:	25
International goals:	3
International trophies:	0
Ballon d'Ors:	0

★ ★ ★ **HERO RATING: 86** ★ ★ ★

VINÍCIUS JÚNIOR
HONOURS

Real Madrid

🏆 FIFA Club World Cup: 2018, 2023

🏆 La Liga: 2019–20, 2021–22

🏆 Spanish Super Cup: 2019–20, 2021–22

🏆 UEFA Champions League: 2021–22

🏆 UEFA Super Cup: 2022

🏆 Copa del Rey Winner: 2023

Brazil

🏆 U-15 South American Championship: 2015

🏆 U-17 South American Championship: 2017

Individual

🏆 South American U-17 Championship Best Player: 2017

🏆 UEFA Champions League Young Player of the Season: 2021–22

🏆 UEFA Champions League Team of the Season: 2021–22

🏆 La Liga Team of the Season: 2021–22

GREATEST MOMENTS

10 AUGUST 2017, FLAMENGO 5–0 PALESTINO

In this Copa Sudamericana match, seventeen-year-old Vinícius came on with twenty minutes to go. Seconds later, he smashed a first-time shot past the goalkeeper to score his first goal for the Flamengo first team. Wow, what a super sub!

2

1 MARCH 2020,
REAL MADRID 2–0 BARCELONA

This was the moment Vinícius first became a Real Madrid hero by starring in the biggest game of all: El Clásico. After dribbling into the Barcelona box, he kept his cool and scored a crucial goal. Yes, his shot deflected off a defender, but who cared about that? Real were winning and they went on to lift the La Liga title that season.

3

12 MAY 2022,
REAL MADRID 6–0 LEVANTE

After three up and down seasons, 2021–22 was Vinícius's breakthrough year. He had already scored two goals many times for Real Madrid, but in this La Liga match against Levante, he finally completed his first hat-trick. A new Brazilian superstar was born.

4 28 MAY 2022, REAL MADRID 1–0 LIVERPOOL

With three goals and seven assists, Vinícius played a key part as Real Madrid reached yet another Champions League final. And in the biggest game of all at the Stade de France in Paris, he stepped up to become the matchwinner. Racing on to Federico Valverde's cross-shot, Vinícius calmly slid in at the back post to score. Hurray, he was the hero!

5 5 DECEMBER 2022, BRAZIL 4–1 SOUTH KOREA

Although the tournament ended in disappointment for Brazil, Vinícius would never forget the moment he scored his first World Cup goal. When the ball came to him, he cushioned it with one touch and dinked a clever finish through a crowd of defenders and into the net. 1–0! After lots of hugs and high-fives, Vinícius danced joyfully in front of the fans with Raphinha and Neymar.

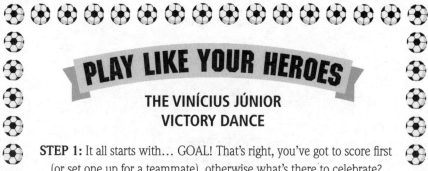

THE VINÍCIUS JÚNIOR VICTORY DANCE

STEP 1: It all starts with… GOAL! That's right, you've got to score first (or set one up for a teammate), otherwise what's there to celebrate?

STEP 2: Once you've watched the ball cross the goal line, ZOOM! Race away towards the corner flag, while kissing the badge on your shirt.

STEP 3: If any of your teammates catch up with you, there's plenty of time for hugs, high-fives and special handshakes first. But if they're still trailing behind, then it's best to move straight on to…

STEP 4: Get the party started! Quick piece of advice here: make sure you practise your dance routine first, before you perform it in front of lots of people. Unless you want to look like a fool!

STEP 5: With a big smile on your face, feel the rhythm flow through your feet, then up to your hips, into your arms, and up to your head. Recommended moves include: hopping, skipping, swinging your hips, crossing your arms over your chest, slicking your hair back, brushing imaginary dirt off your shoulders, swinging an invisible lasso like a cowboy, and my personal favourite, pretending to make two phone calls at the same time. Whatever you want, basically!

STEP 6: Try to get as many teammates as possible to do the dance with you. If it's a really big goal, maybe you could even ask your manager to join in. The more the merrier!

TEST YOUR KNOWLEDGE

QUESTIONS

1. What was the name of the coach who first spotted Vinícius's one-of-a-kind talent at the age of seven?

2. Playing which other sport helped Vinícius to become even more skilful on the ball?

3. Who did Vinícius go to live with to be closer to the Flamengo academy?

4. As a boy, Vinícius had a picture of which Brazilian star on his bedroom wall?

5. Vinícius scored his first goal for the Flamengo first team against which club?

6. How old was Vinícius when he left Brazil to move to Madrid?

7. Which Brazilian legend was there at the Bernabéu to welcome Vinícius to Real Madrid?

8. Whose record did Vinícius beat to become the youngest ever goalscorer in El Clásico?

9. Which two amazing managers has Vinícius worked under at Real Madrid?

10. Vinícius scored the winning goal in the 2022 Champions League final, but who set him up?

11. At the 2022 World Cup in Qatar, Vinícius scored his only goal against which team?

11. *South Korea.*
9. *Zinedine Zidane and Carlo Ancelotti.* 10. *Federico Valverde.*
4. *Robinho.* 5. *Palestino.* 6. *Eighteen.* 7. *Ronaldo.* 8. *Lionel Messi's.*
1. *Cacau.* 2. *Futsal.* 3. *His uncle Ulysses and aunt Tatiana.*

175

CAN'T GET ENOUGH OF ULTIMATE FOOTBALL HEROES?

Check out heroesfootball.com
for quizzes, games, and competitions!

Plus join the Ultimate Football Heroes
Fan Club to score exclusive content
and be the first to hear about
new books and events.
heroesfootball.com/subscribe/